COLOR

Egyptian art
Phoenician Art

Conceived, Designed, and Illustrated by:
Mrinal Mitra

Series edited by:
Swarna Mitra & **Malika Mitra**

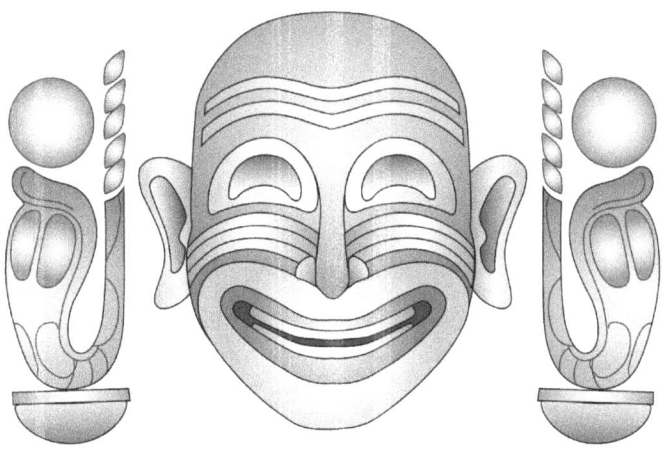

This series is dedicated to the citizens of the world;
from the young blooming minds of children, to the aspired individuals of all ages.

COLOR
Egyptian art

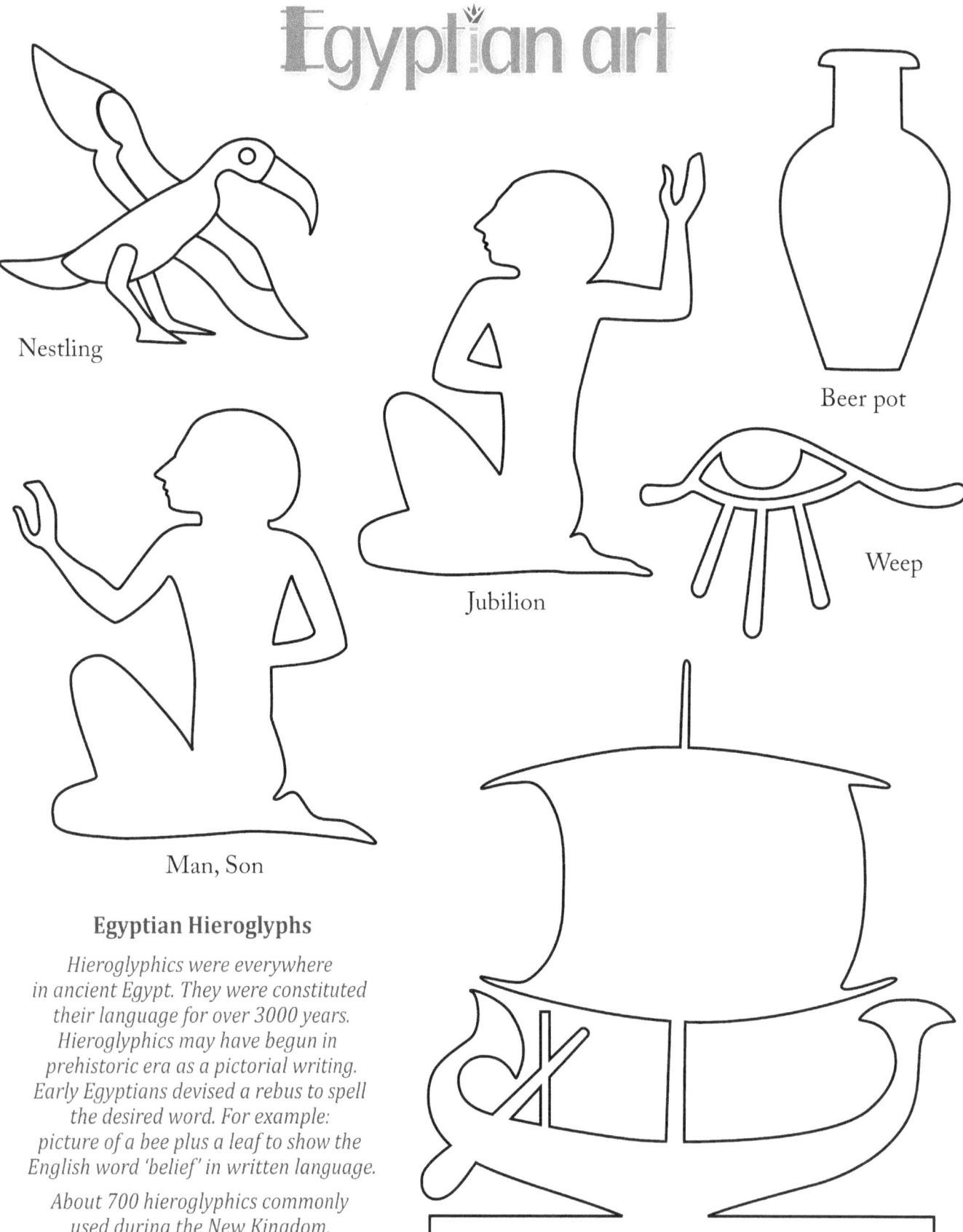

Nestling

Beer pot

Jubilion

Weep

Man, Son

Egyptian Hieroglyphs

Hieroglyphics were everywhere in ancient Egypt. They were constituted their language for over 3000 years. Hieroglyphics may have begun in prehistoric era as a pictorial writing. Early Egyptians devised a rebus to spell the desired word. For example: picture of a bee plus a leaf to show the English word 'belief' in written language.

About 700 hieroglyphics commonly used during the New Kingdom, at least 100 remained strictly visual.

Sail, upstream

Egyptian Hieroglyphs

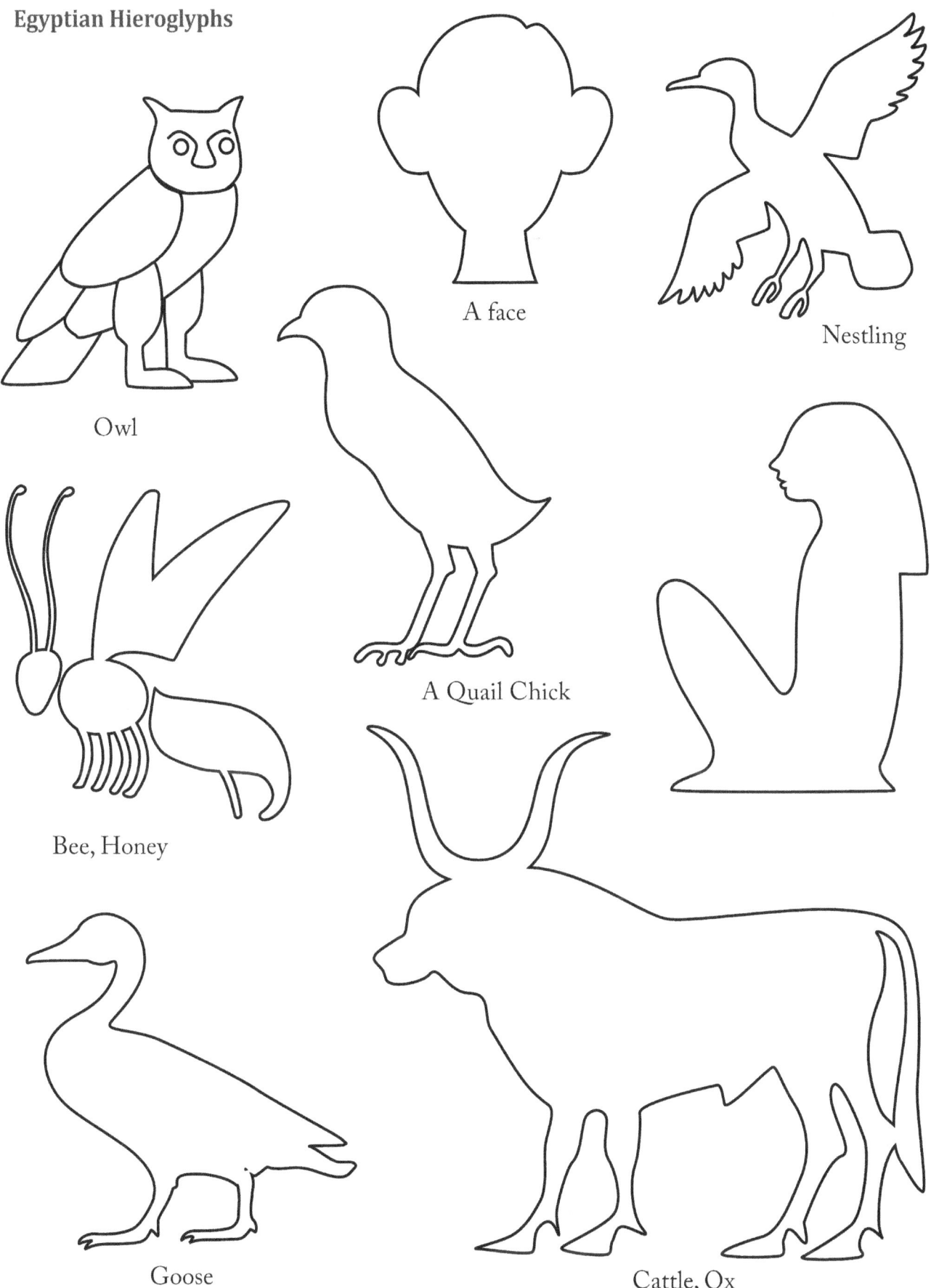

Owl

A face

Nestling

A Quail Chick

Bee, Honey

Goose

Cattle, Ox

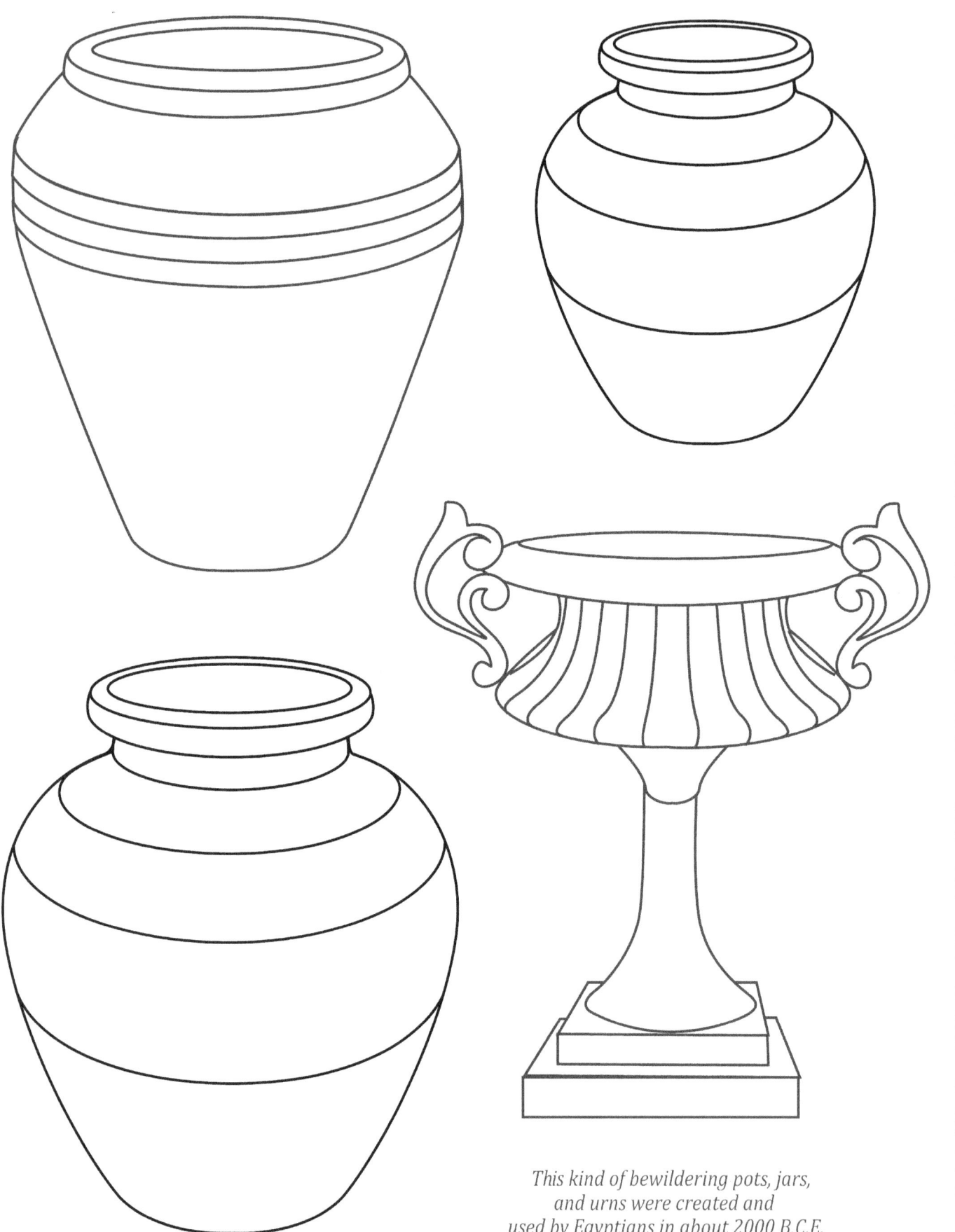

This kind of bewildering pots, jars, and urns were created and used by Egyptians in about 2000 B.C.E.

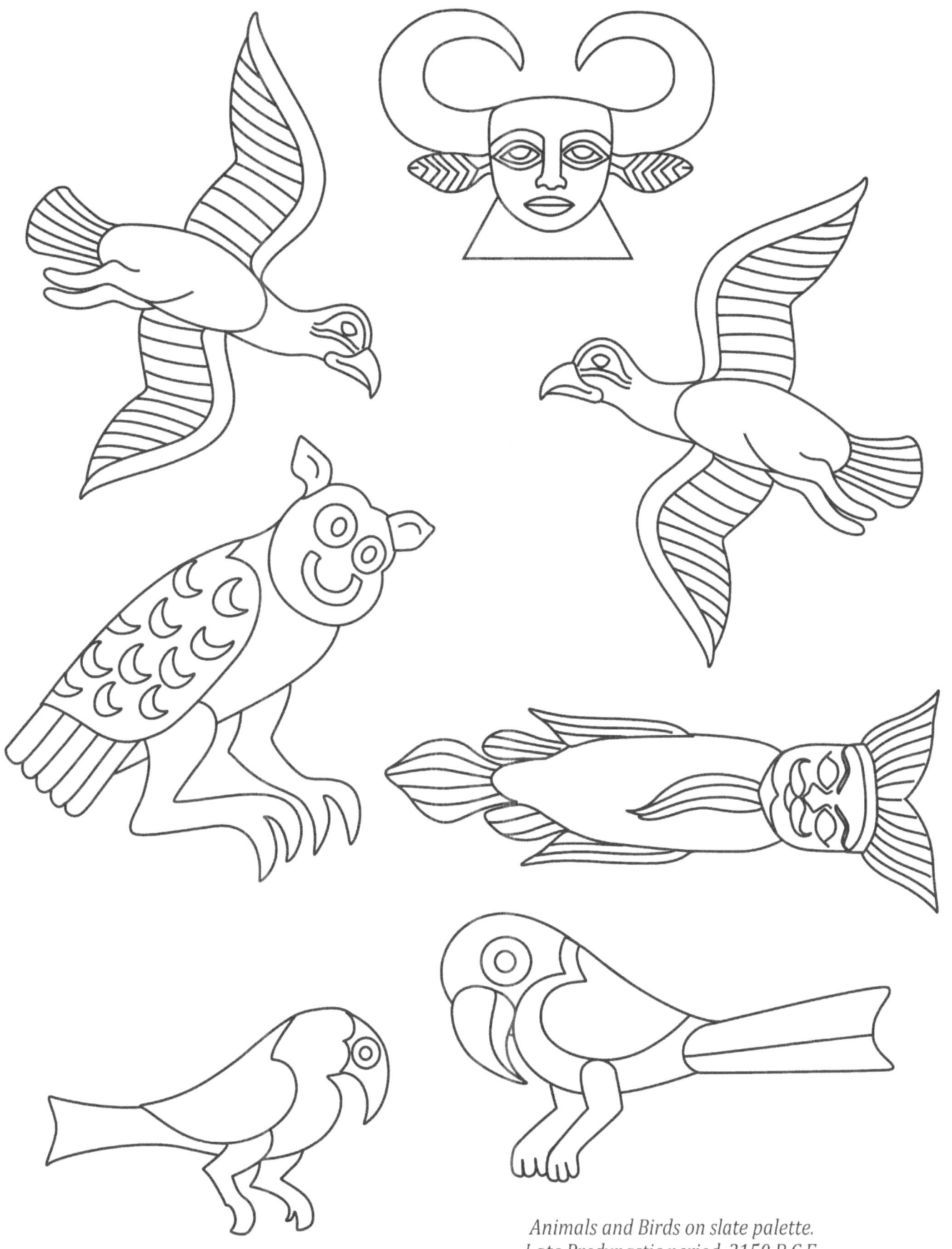

Animals and Birds on slate palette.
Late Predynastic period, 3150 B.C.E.

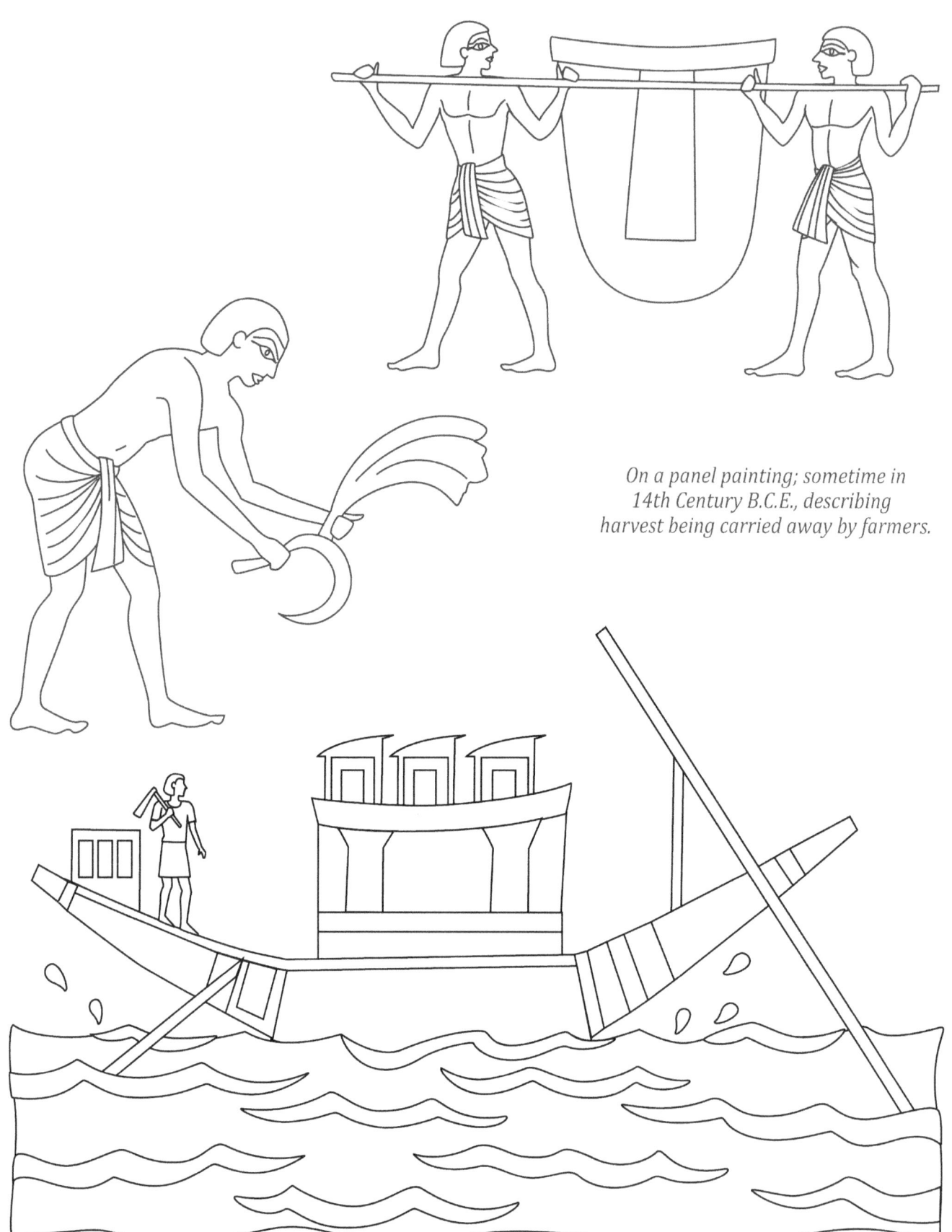

*On a panel painting; sometime in
14th Century B.C.E., describing
harvest being carried away by farmers.*

From a panel painting sometime in 14th Century B.C.E., describing harvest being transported by boat.

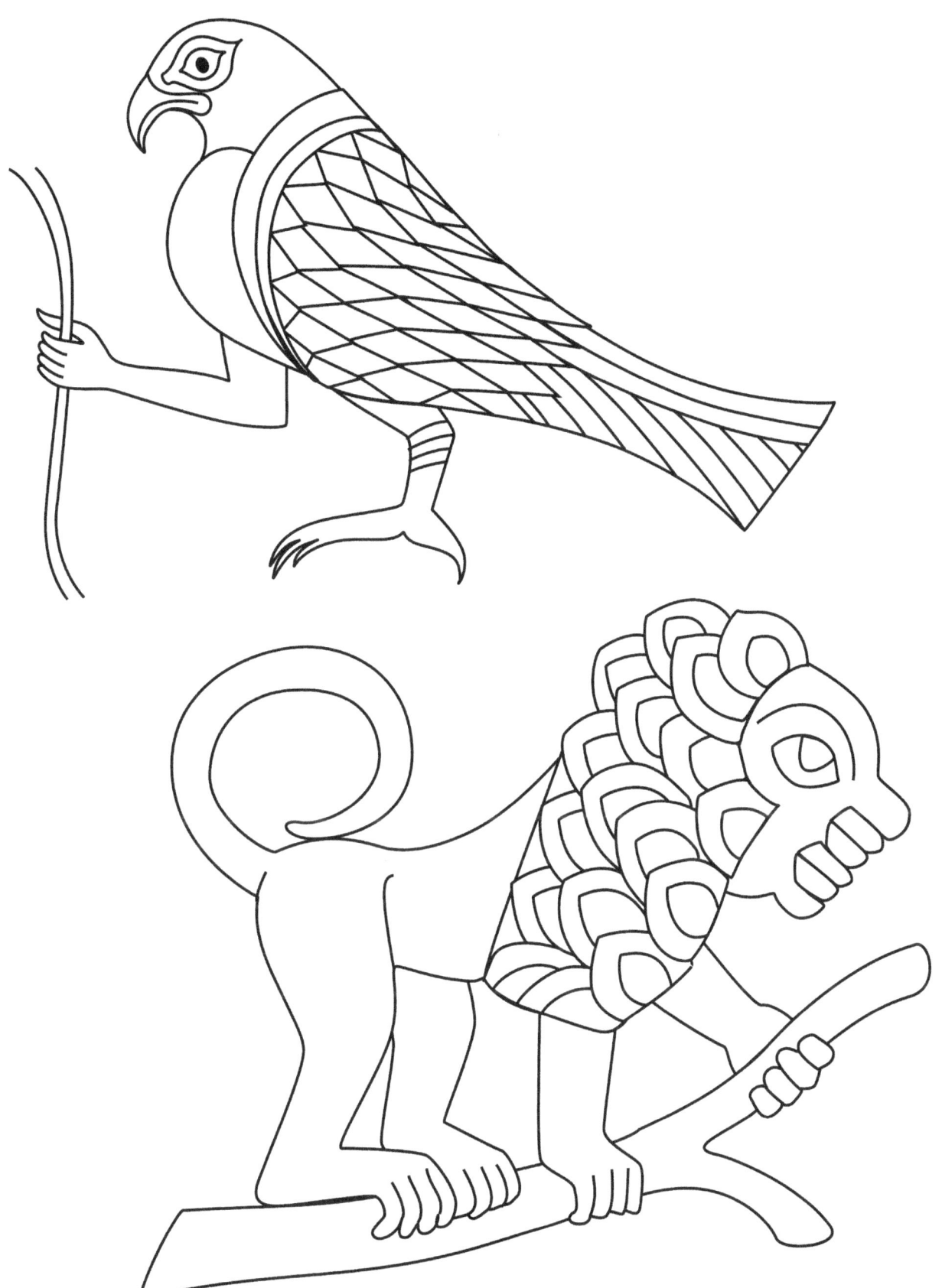

Animals and birds on slate palette in the grave of late Predynastic period, 3100 B.C.E.

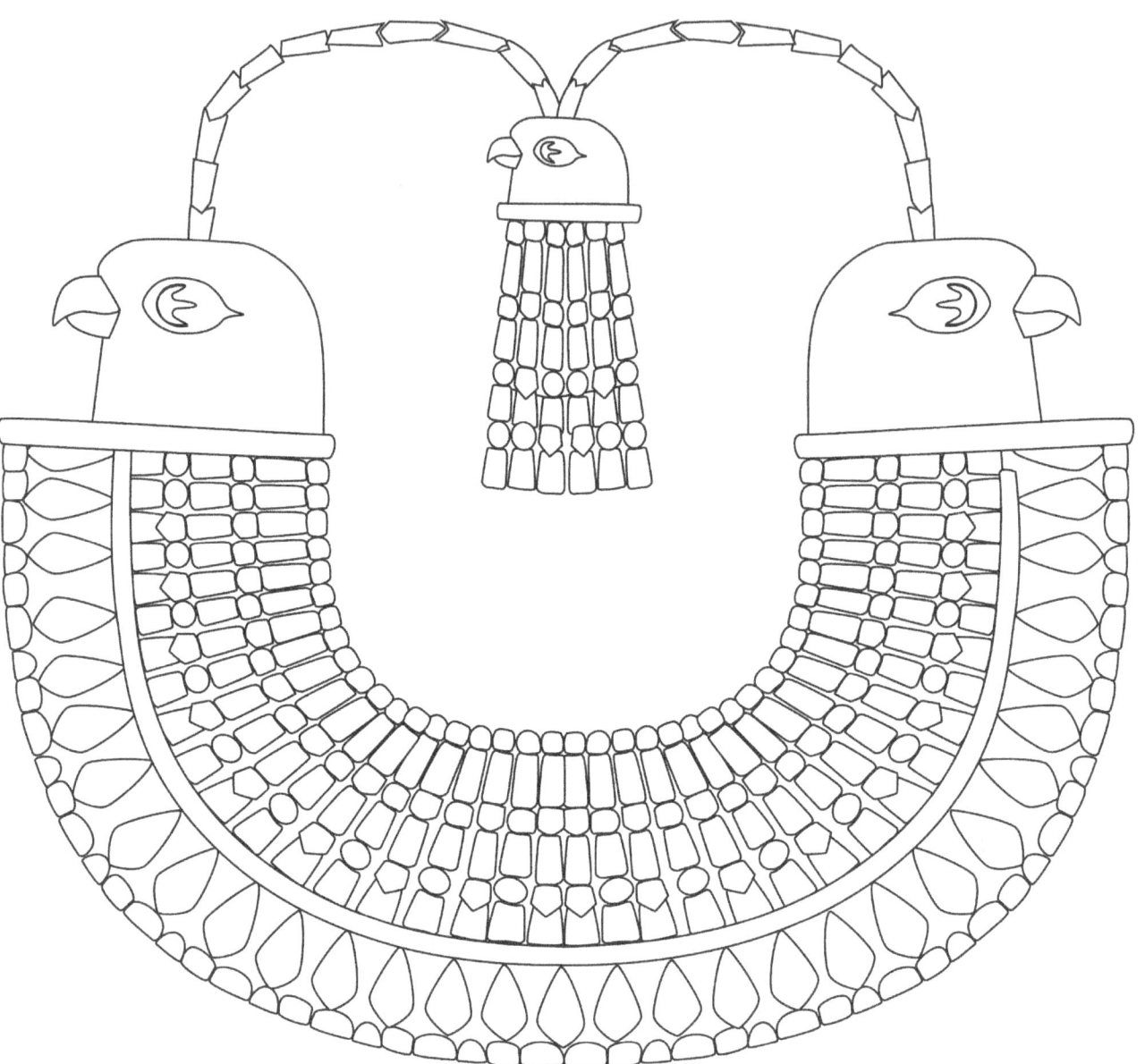

A necklace with falcon head on both sides. The beads
are made of glass, calcite, lapis lazuli, and electrum.
In the centre, is a counter weight, used at the back
of heavy necklace to keep them in place.
Found in Tutankhamun's tomb.

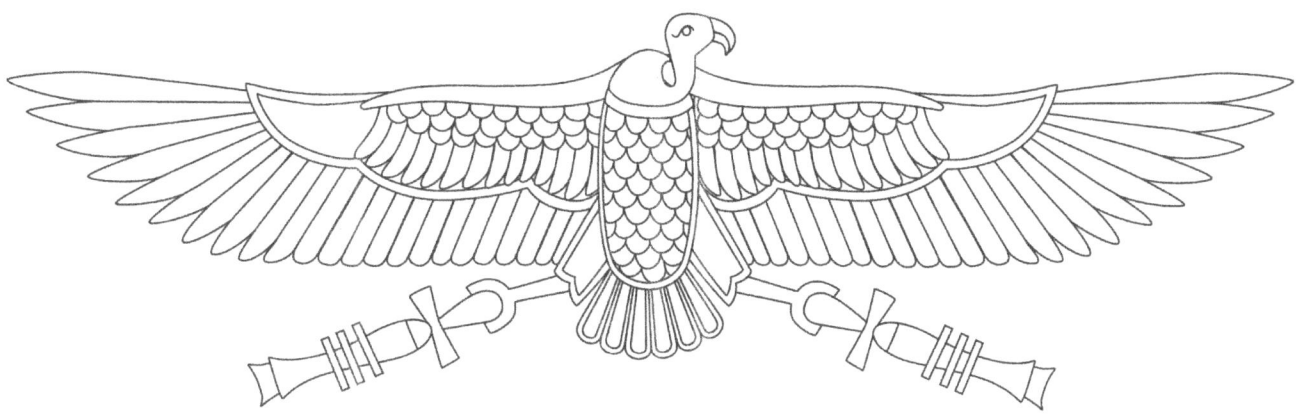

Symbol of Nekhbet vulture, the motif is developed reflecting from burial treasure of princess Mererel.

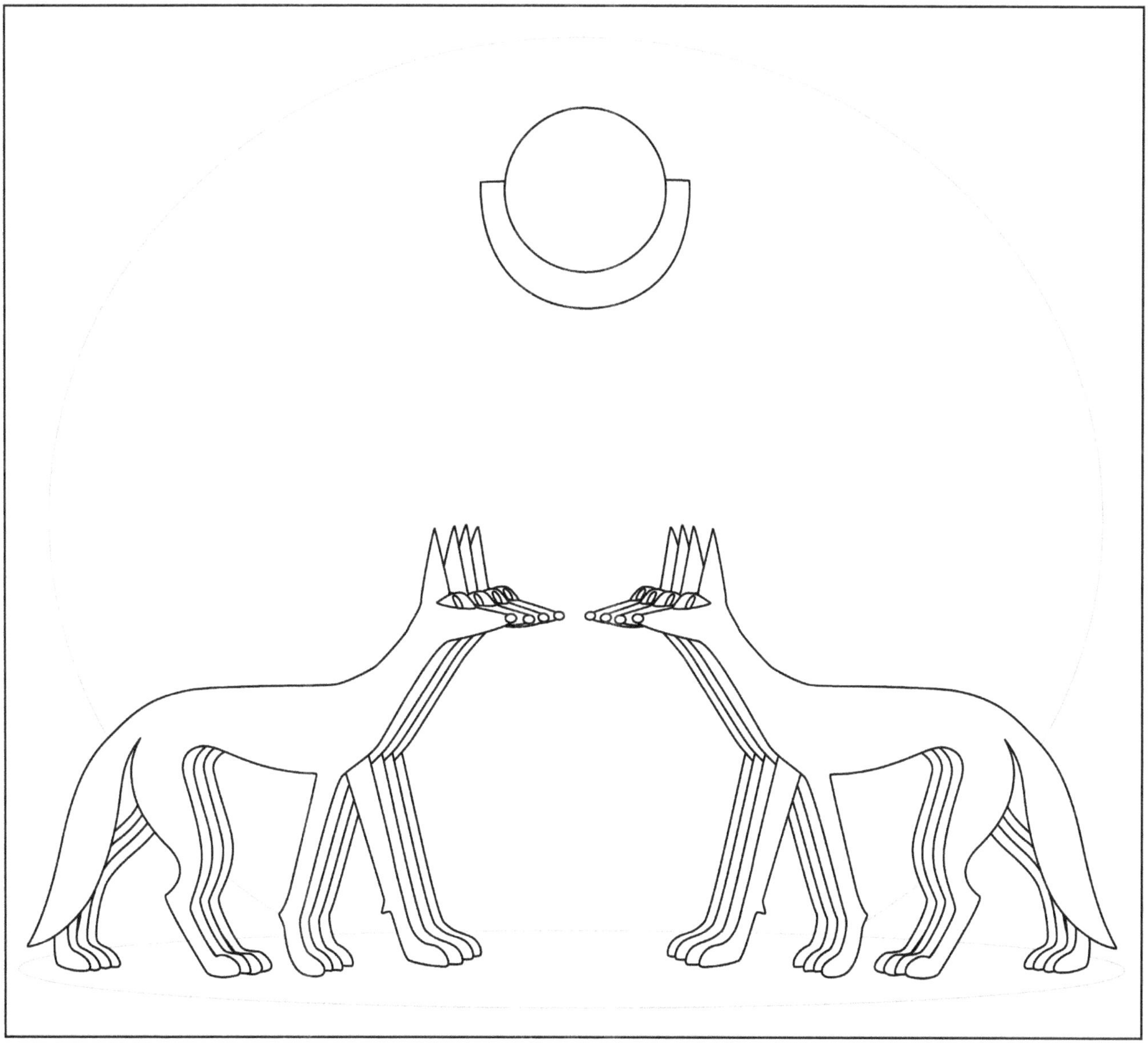

Jackals in a row from an Egyptian painting in the temple. On top placed Egyptian Sun disc. Circa 2000 B.C.E.

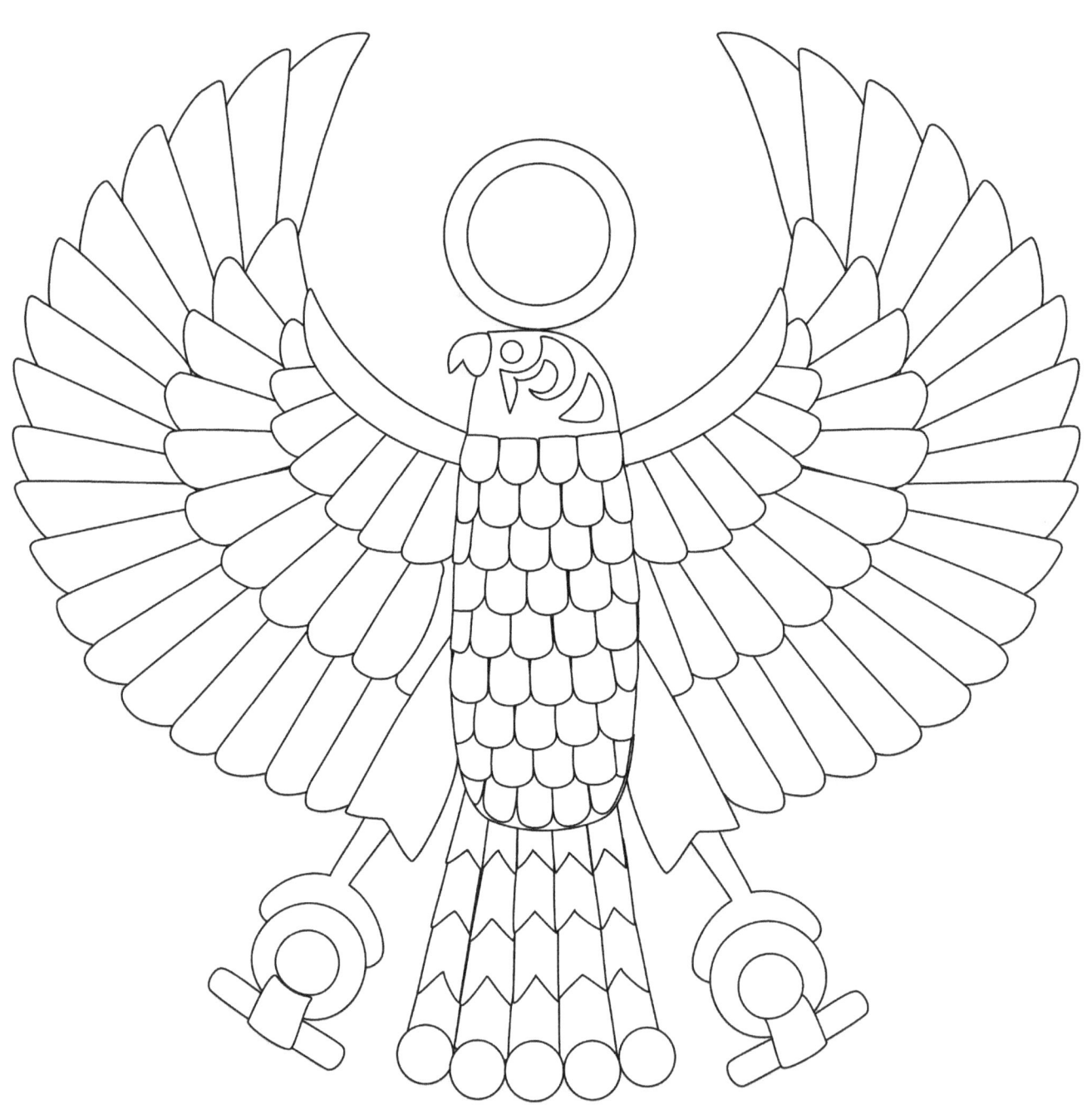

Falcon Pendant.
During Tutankhamun's reign. 1332 - 1323 B.C.E.

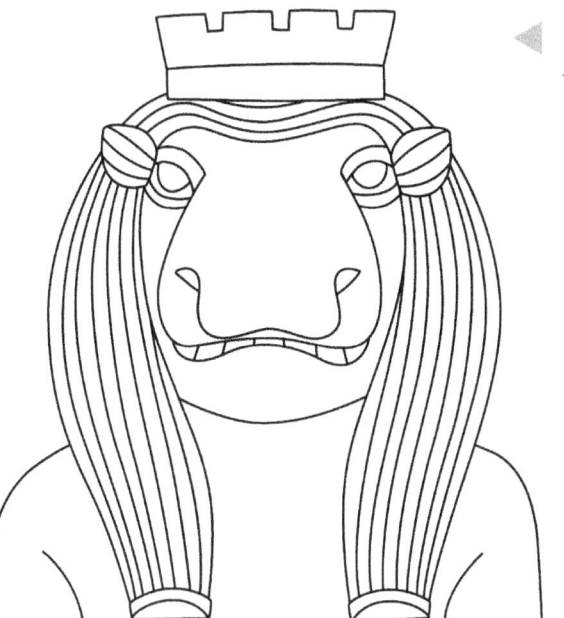

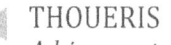 THOUERIS
A hippopotamus, ensured fertility and safe childbirth.

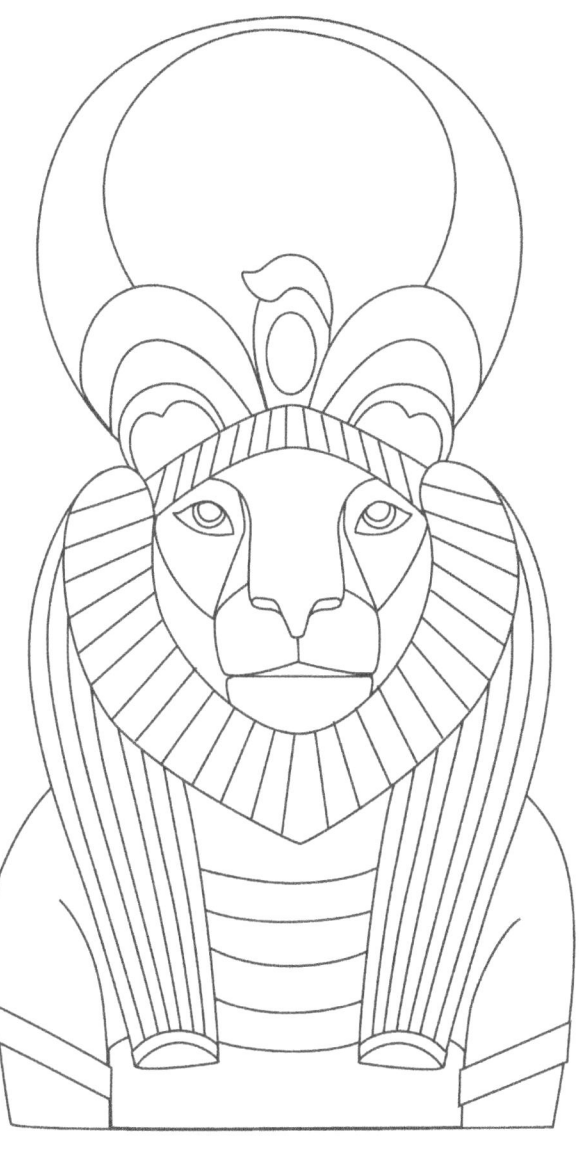

SEKHMET
▲ *War goddess- a part woman and part lioness.*

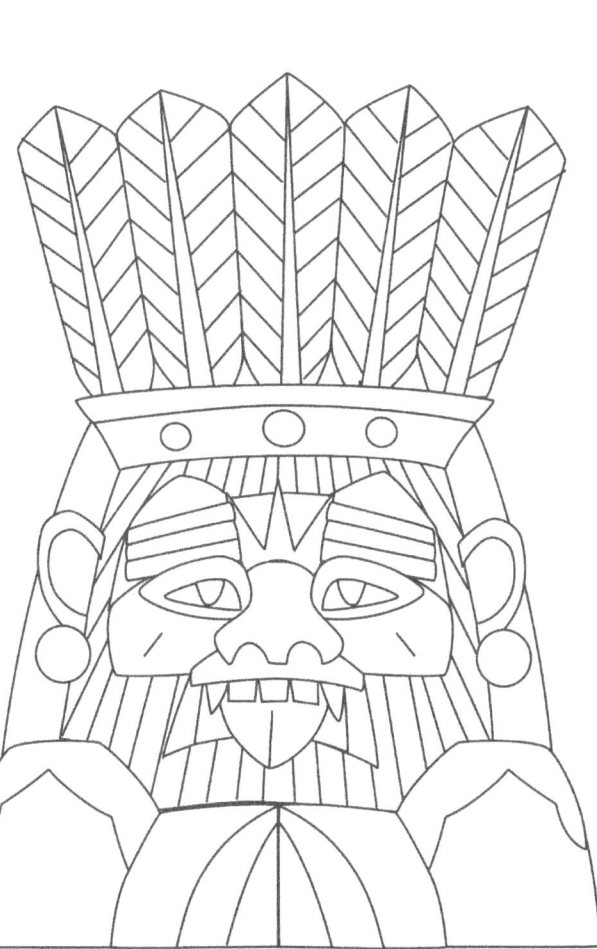

BES
▲ *A lion-headed dwarf, scared off the evil spirits.*

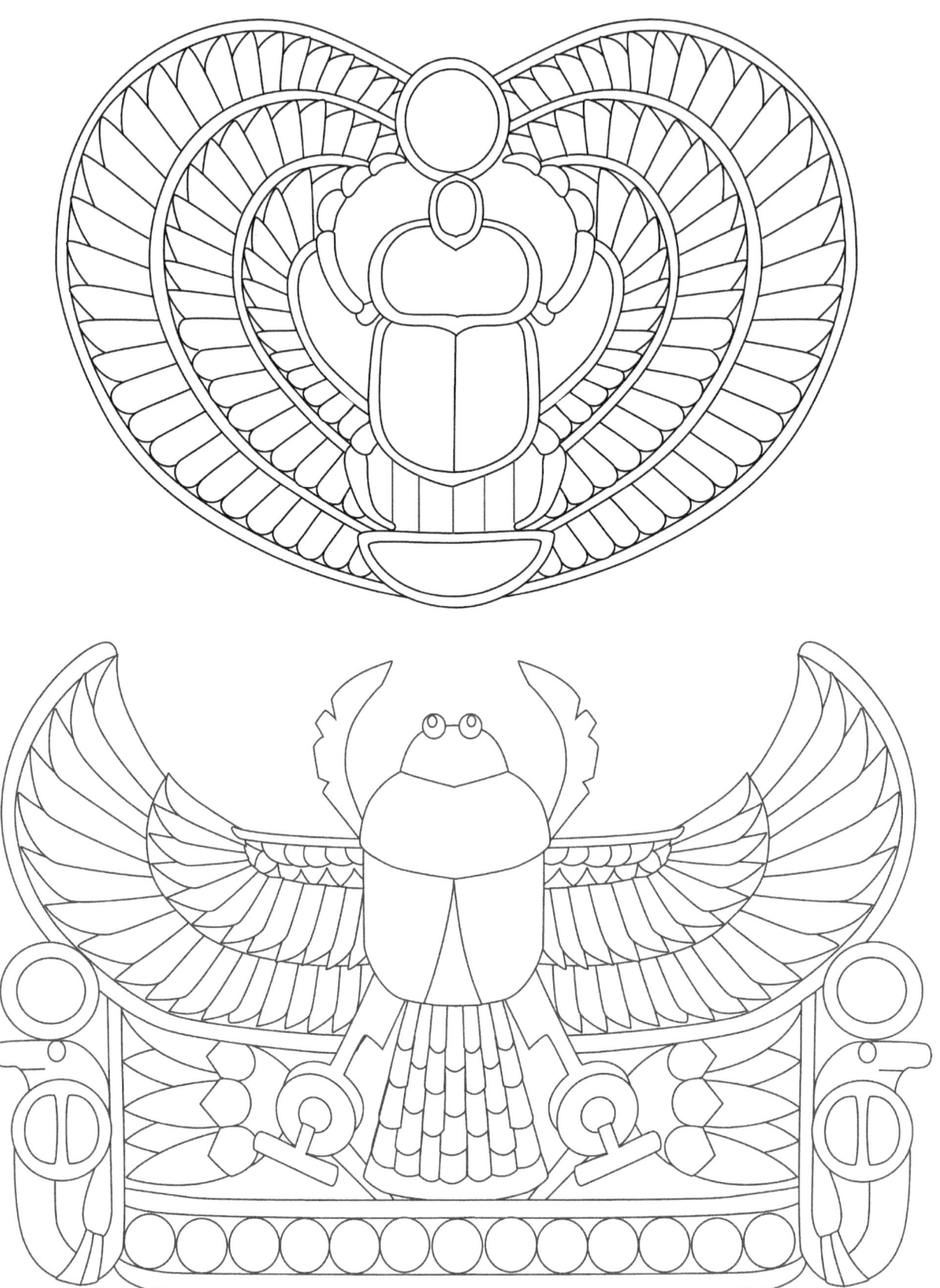

Jewelry, bearing scarab. Many similar ornaments found in Tutankhamun's tomb. 1332 - 1323 B.C.E.

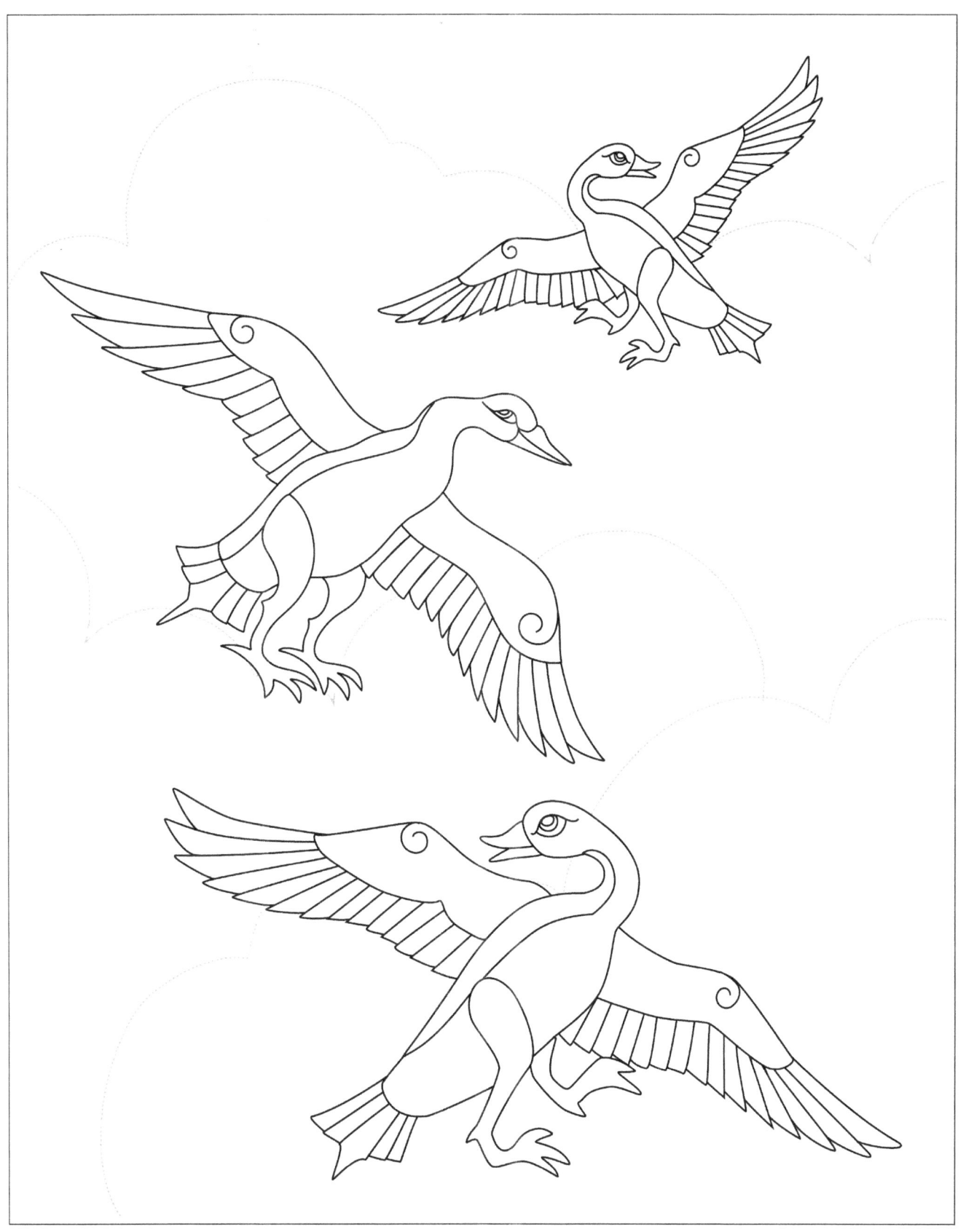

*Flying birds from painting on stucco. New Kingdom,
Eighteenth Dynasty, 1400 B.C.E. From the tomb of Nebamun at Thebes.*

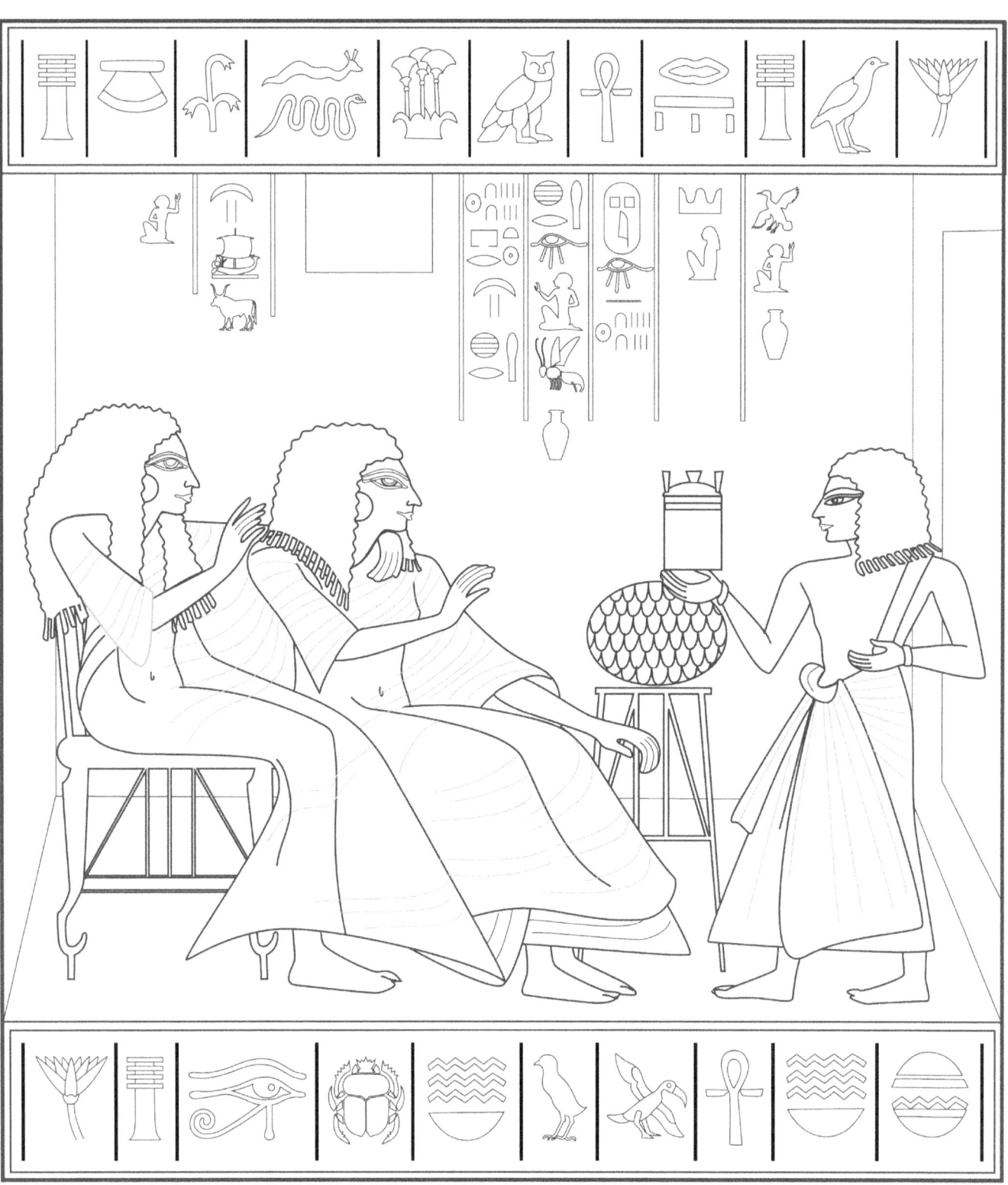

From an ancient tomb painting showing a bereaved family. A departed official's son offering votive gifts.

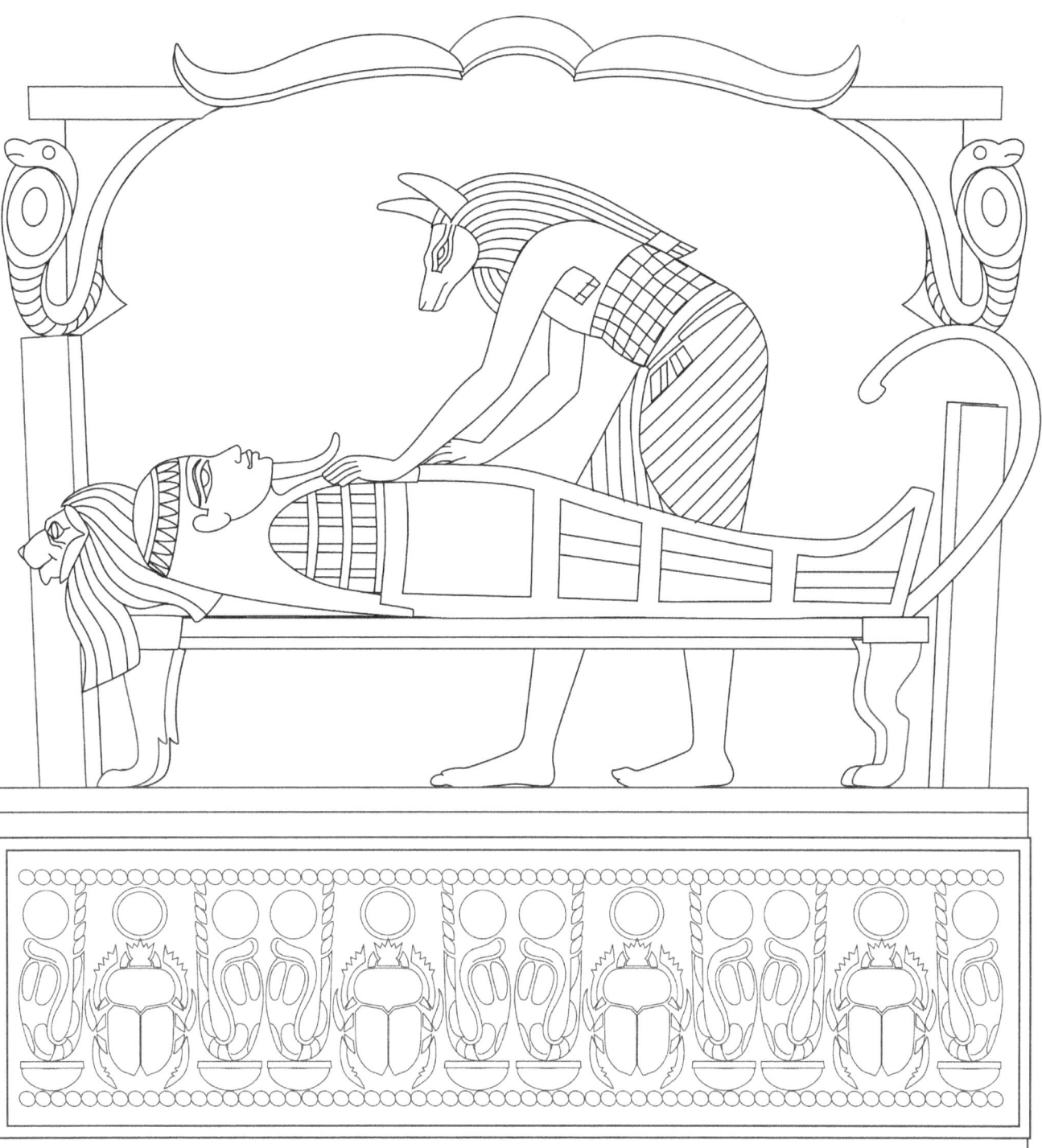

The body of a deceased man is embalmed and prepared
for the tomb by Anubis, the protector of the dead. The body is lying on a lion-headed bier.

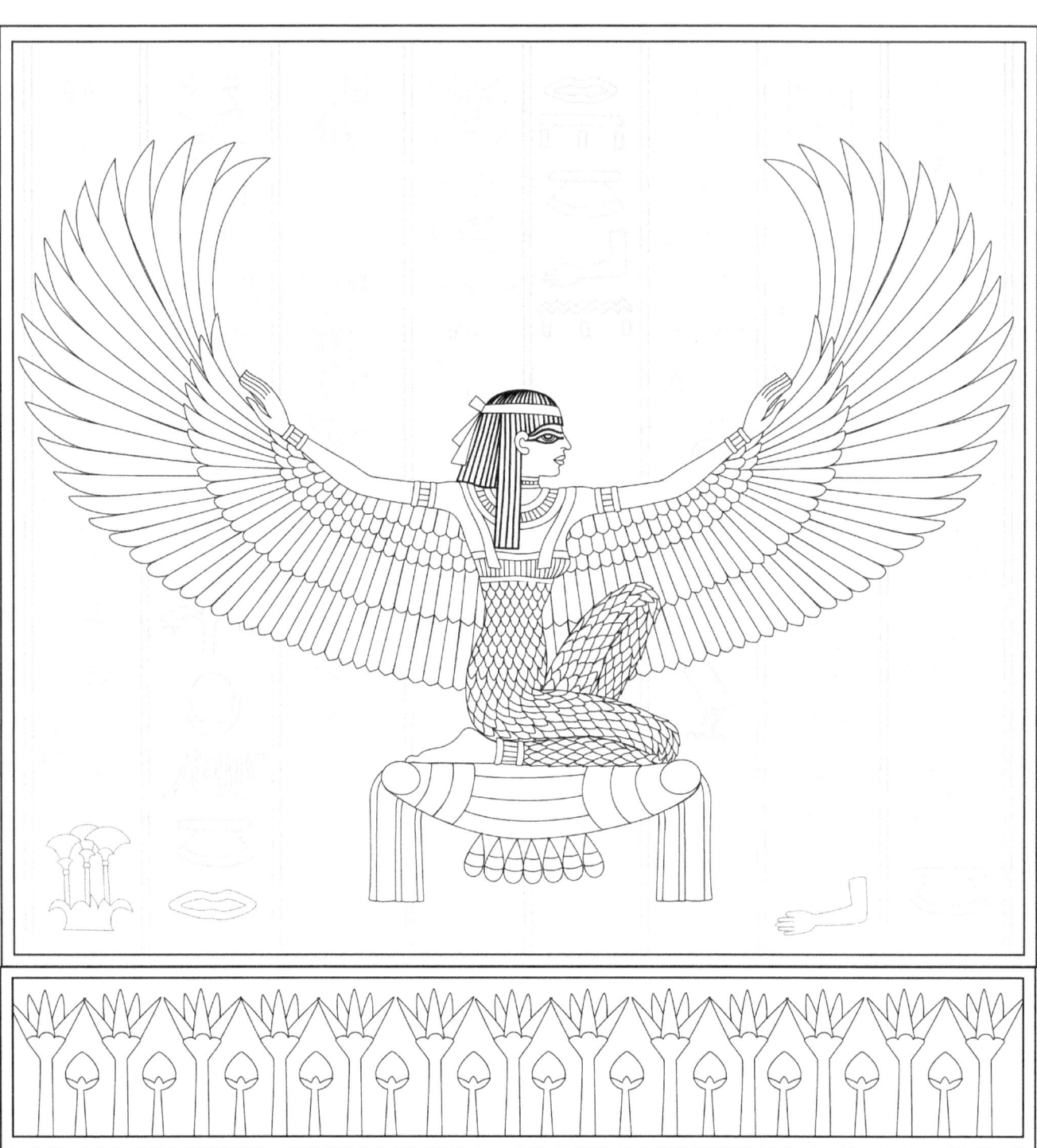

An image of the winged goddess Isis, chased with delicacy and skill beneath the foot of Tutankhamun's innermost gold coffin.

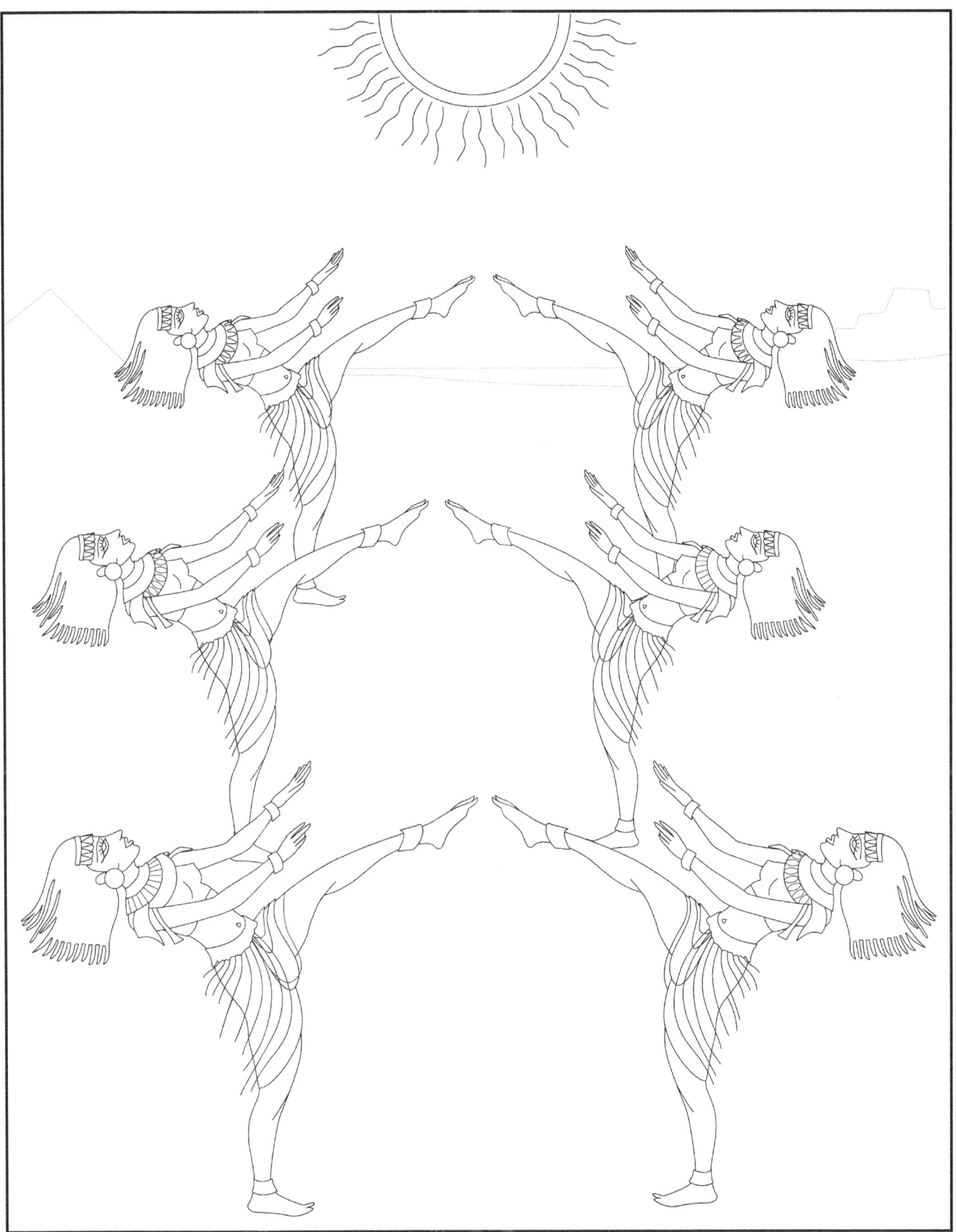

Dancing girls. Painted on plaster. Thebes, Eighteenth Dynasty, Circa 1425 B.C.E.

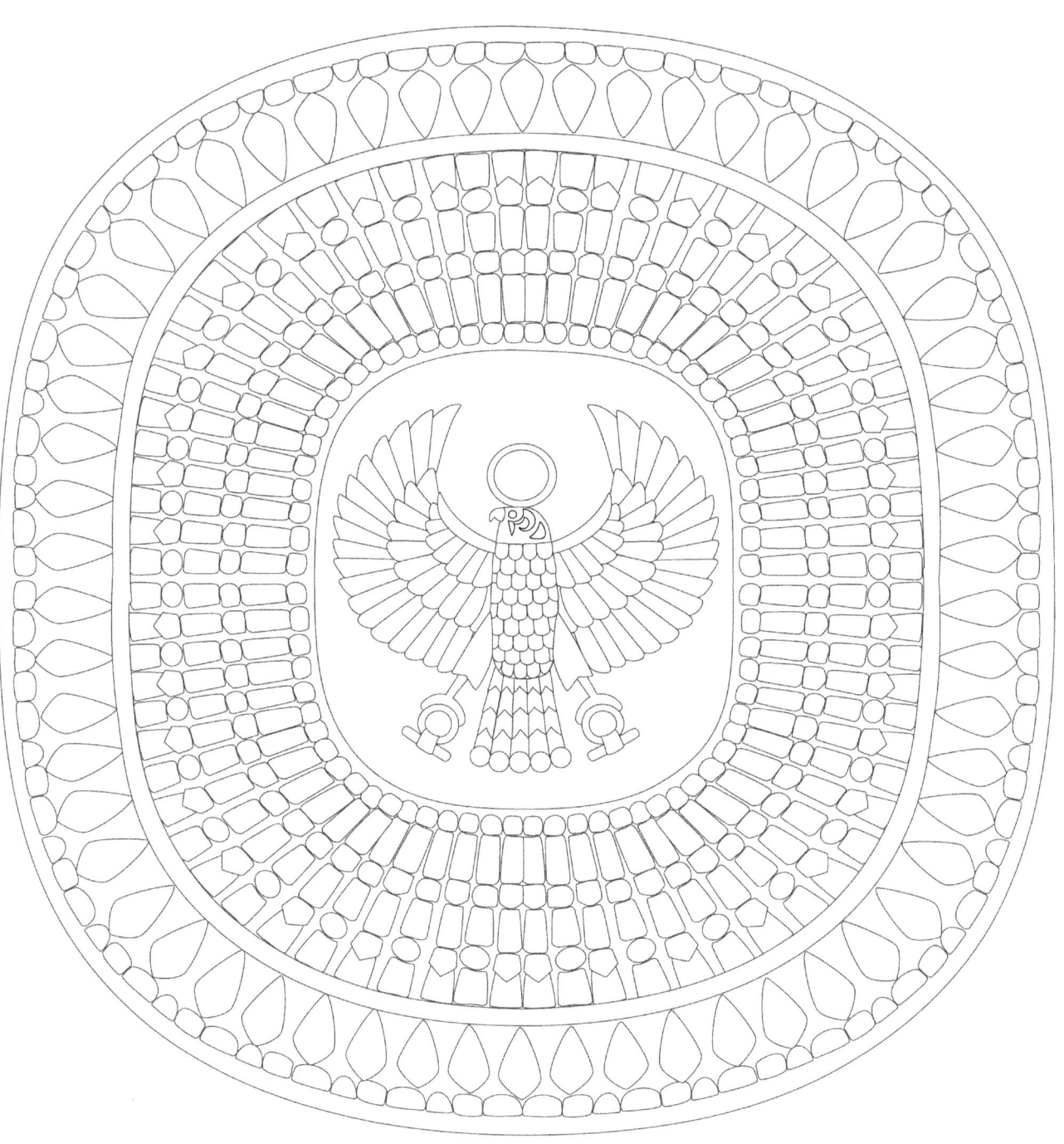

Using these images as examples, create your own piece using the elements found in Egyptian Art.

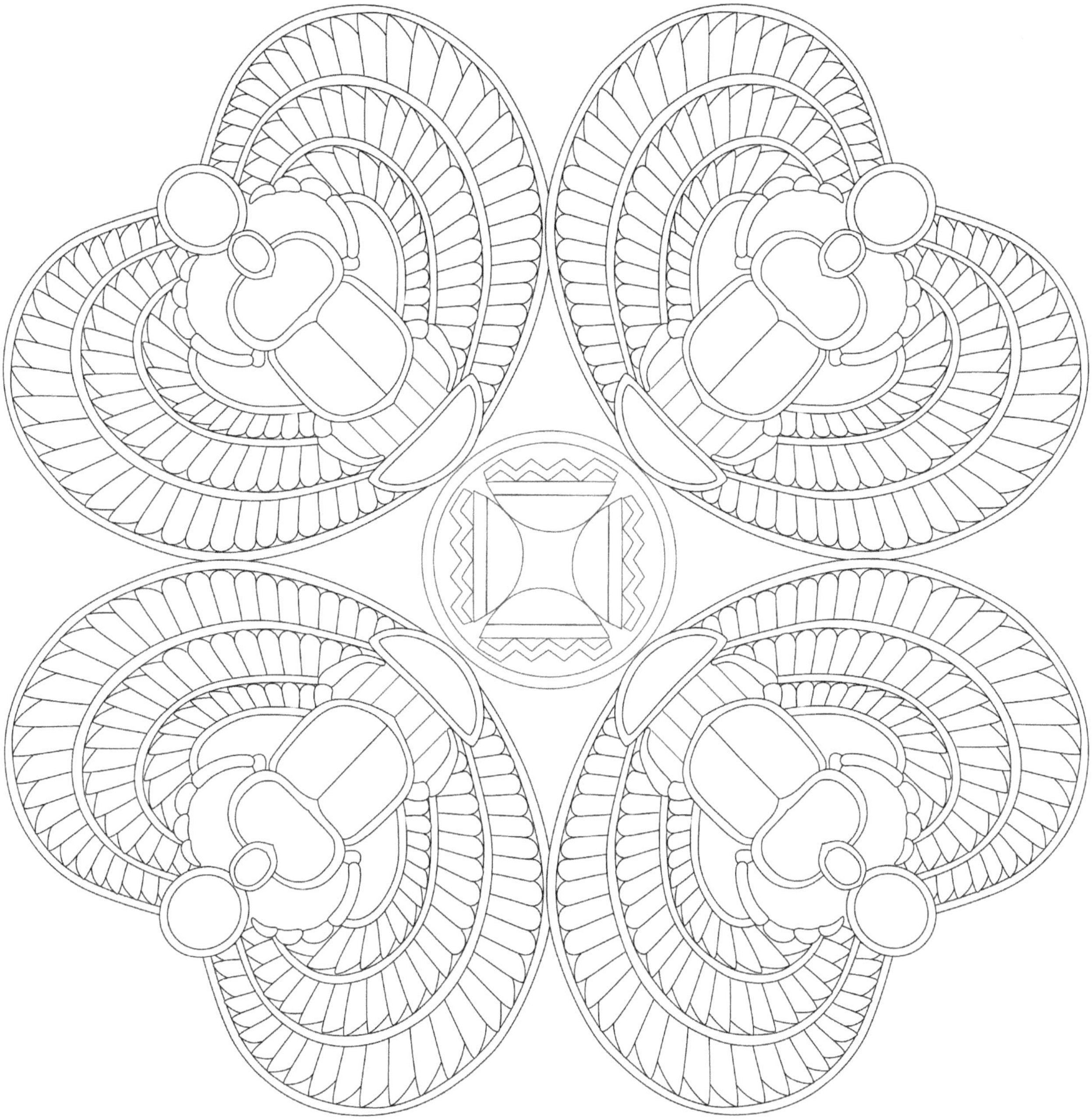

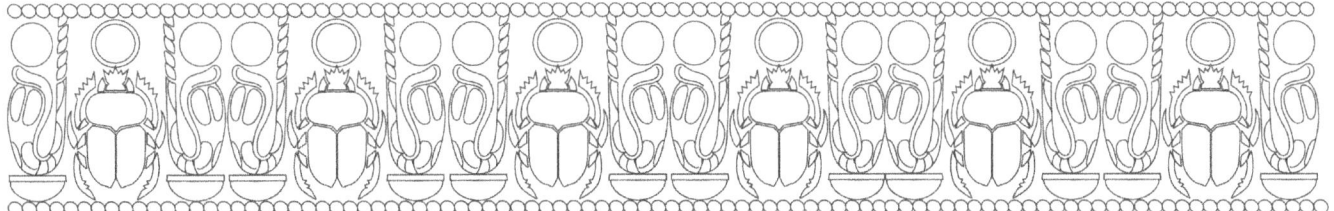

Using these images as examples, create your own piece using the elements found in Egyptian Art.

COLOR
Phoenician Art

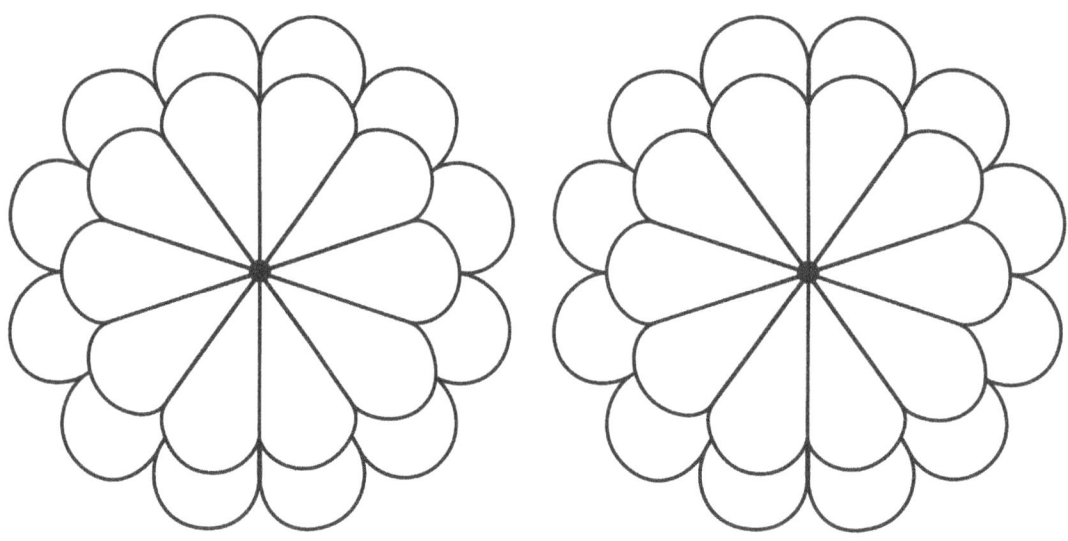

Amulet depicting cippus from Sardinia. 6th - 4th Century B.C.E.

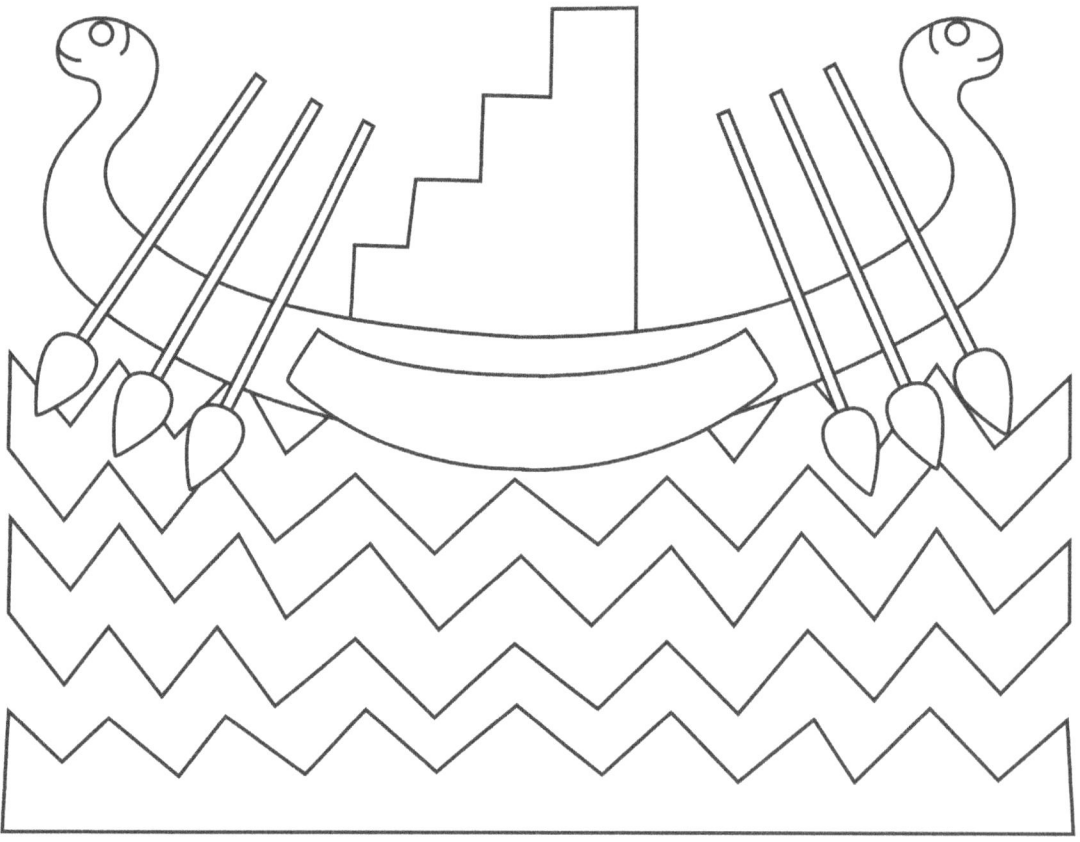

Embossed on a Phoenician coin showing a ship. 5th - 4th Century B.C.E.

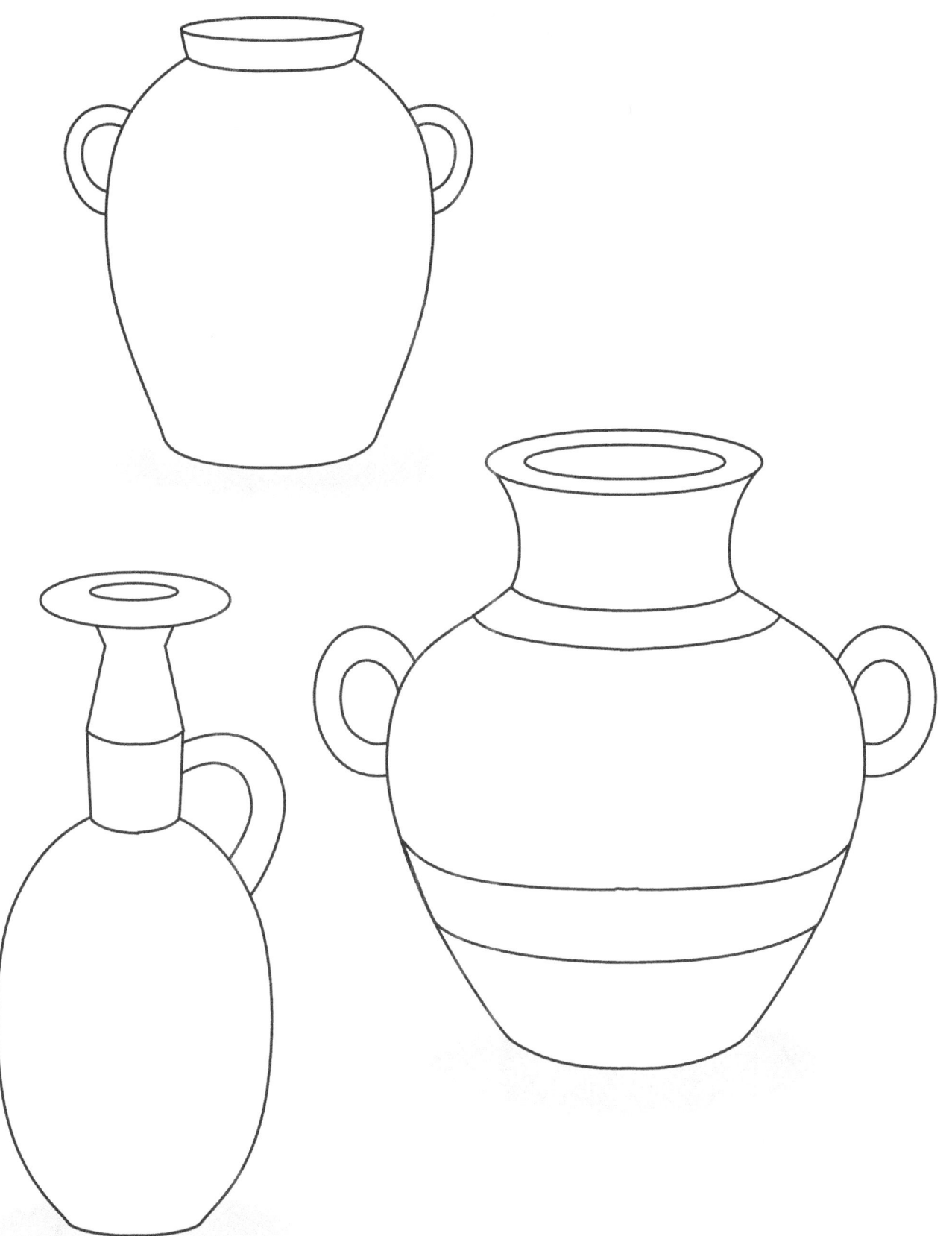

Mashroom lipped jug and Amphoras. 6th Century B.C.E.

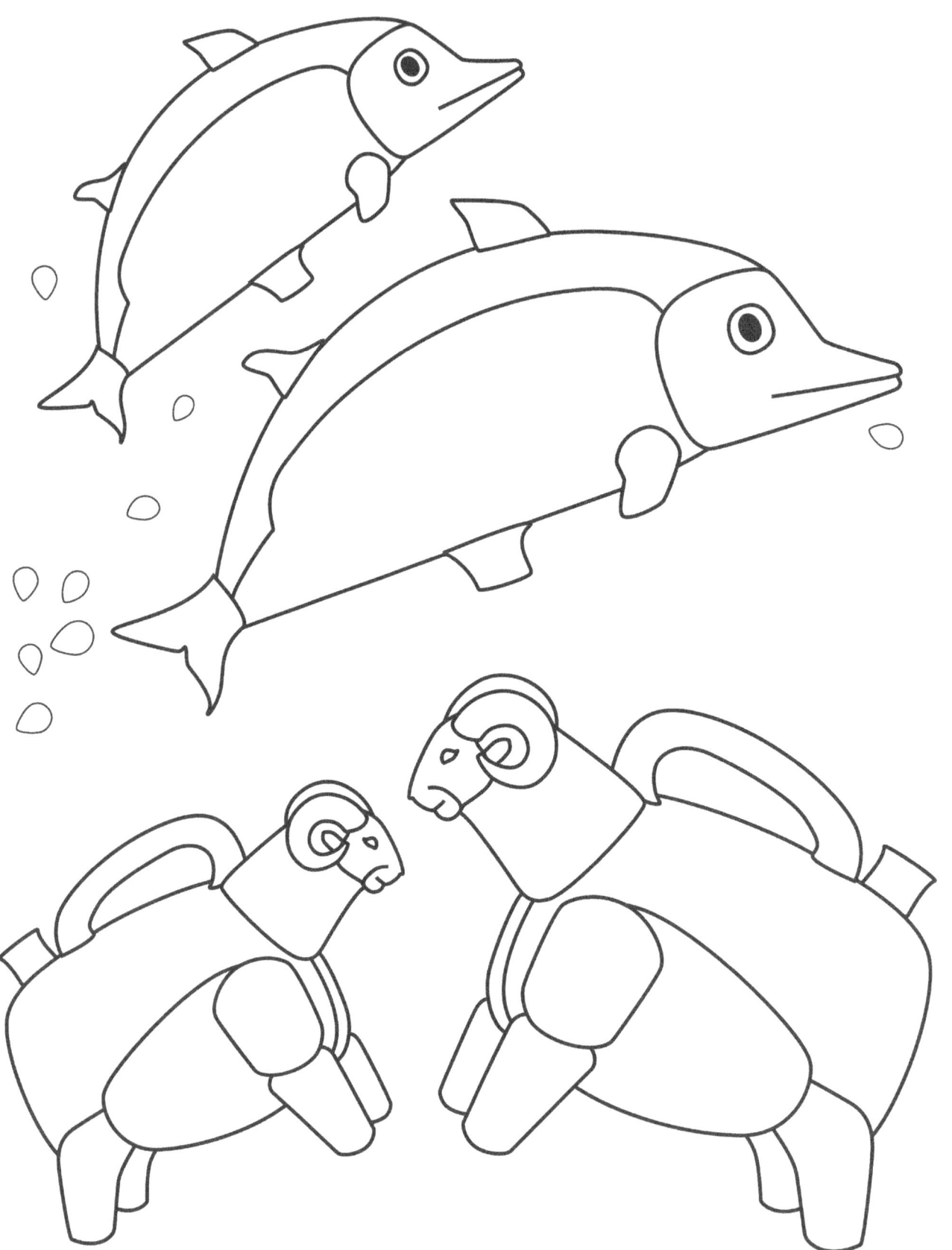

Askos in the form of Dolphin and Ram. Carthage, 4th - 3rd Century B.C.E.

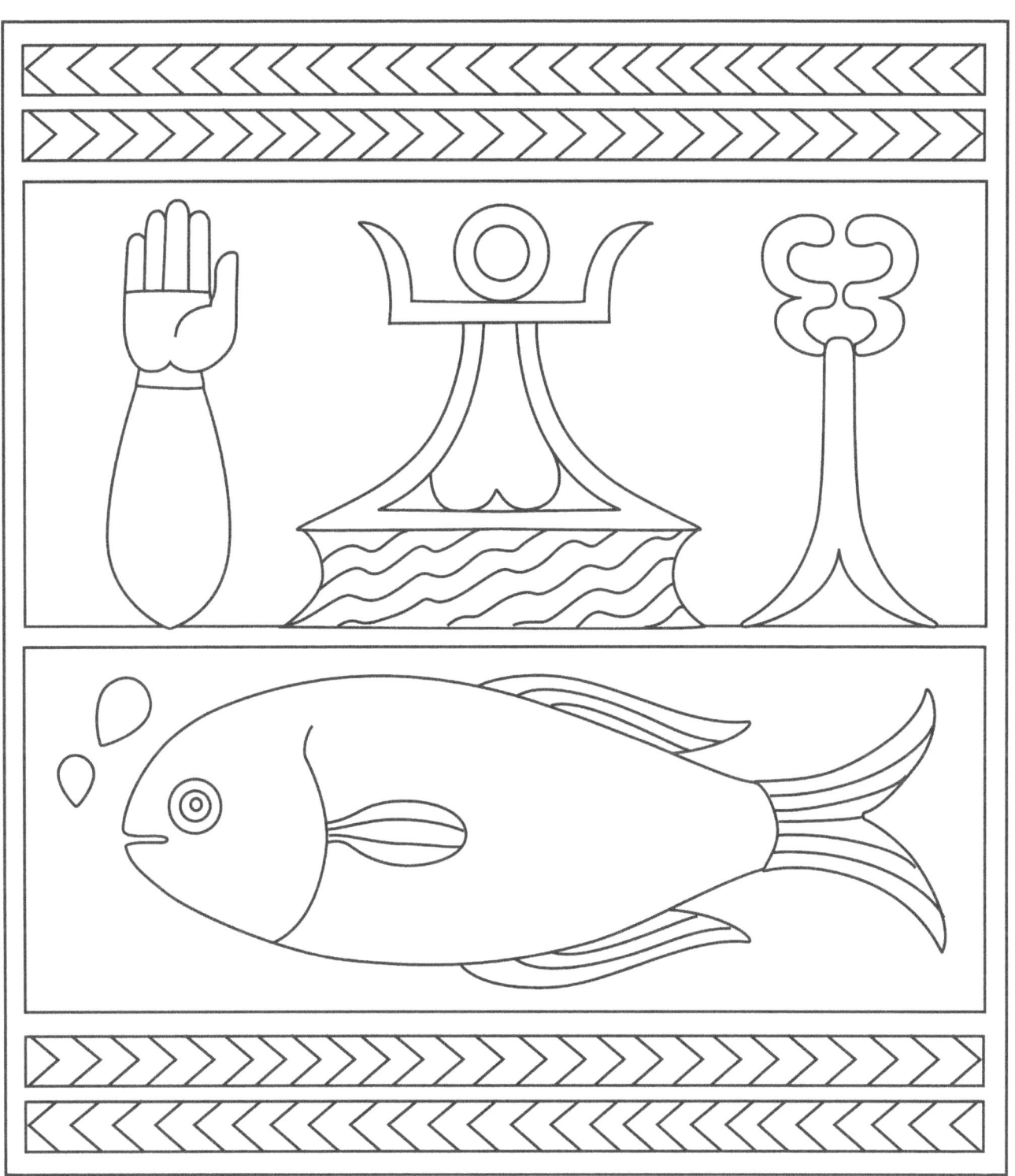

A Phoenician inscription gives the name of the offer on a stele dates back to 3rd or 2nd Century B.C.E.

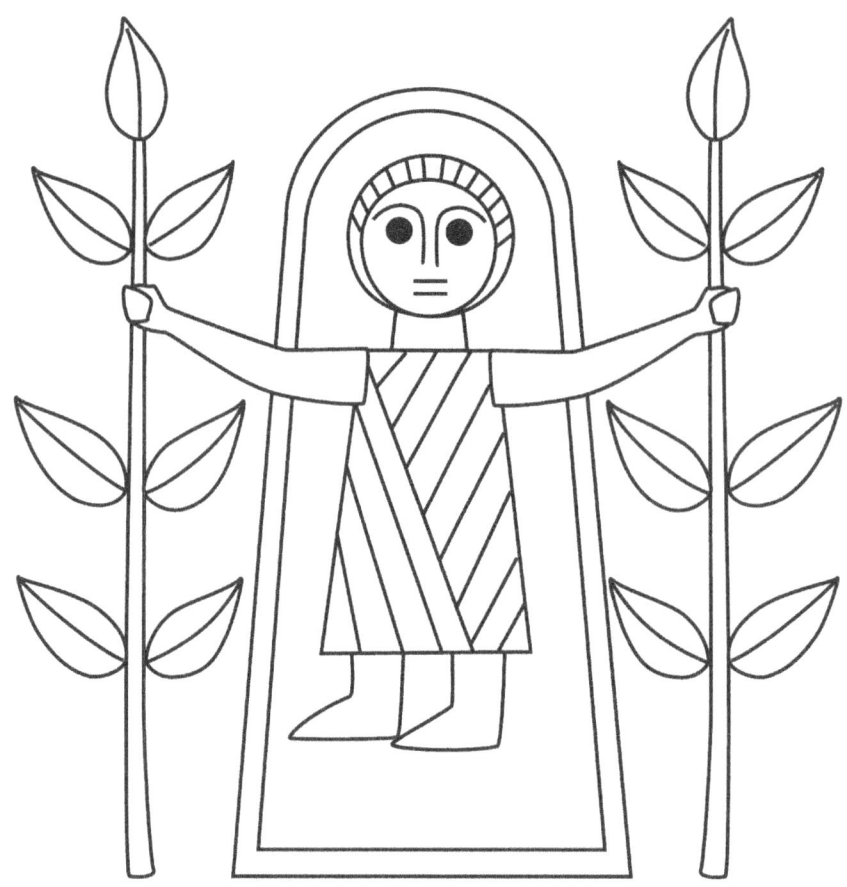

Stele is featuring figure inside niche with foliate motifs. 1st Century B.C.E.

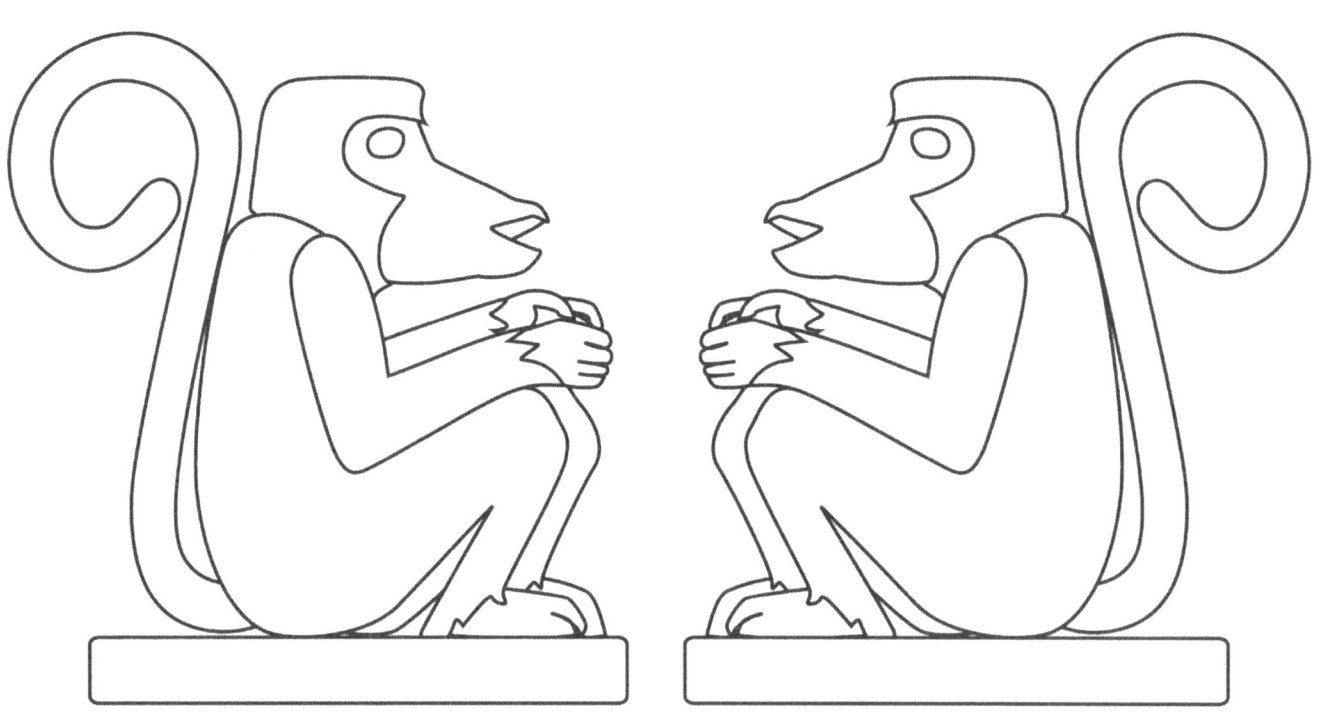

Amulet depicting monkey. Tharros, 5th - 4th Century, B.C.E.

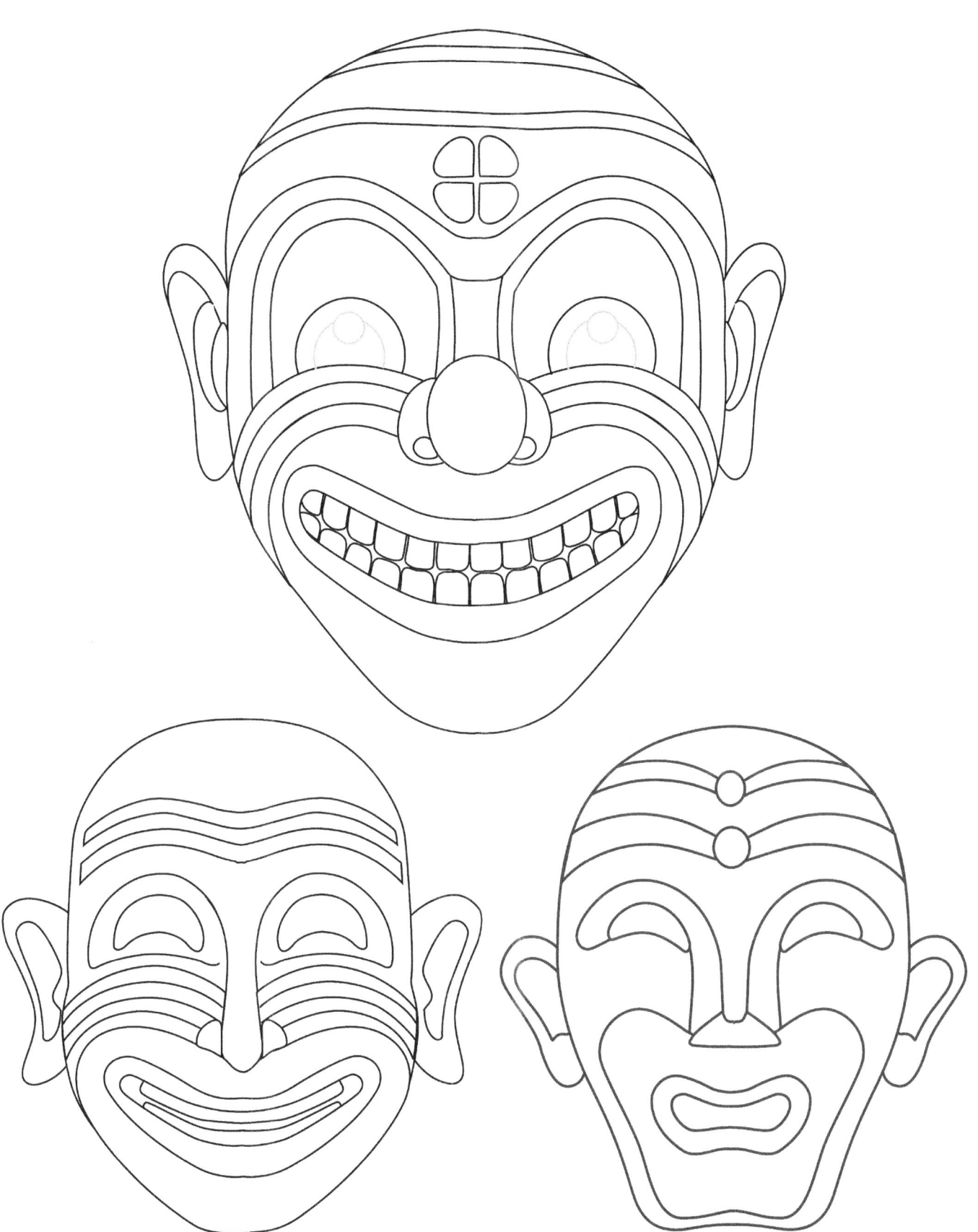

Terracotta grinning masks from Motya and Sansepolcro. 6th Century B.C.E.

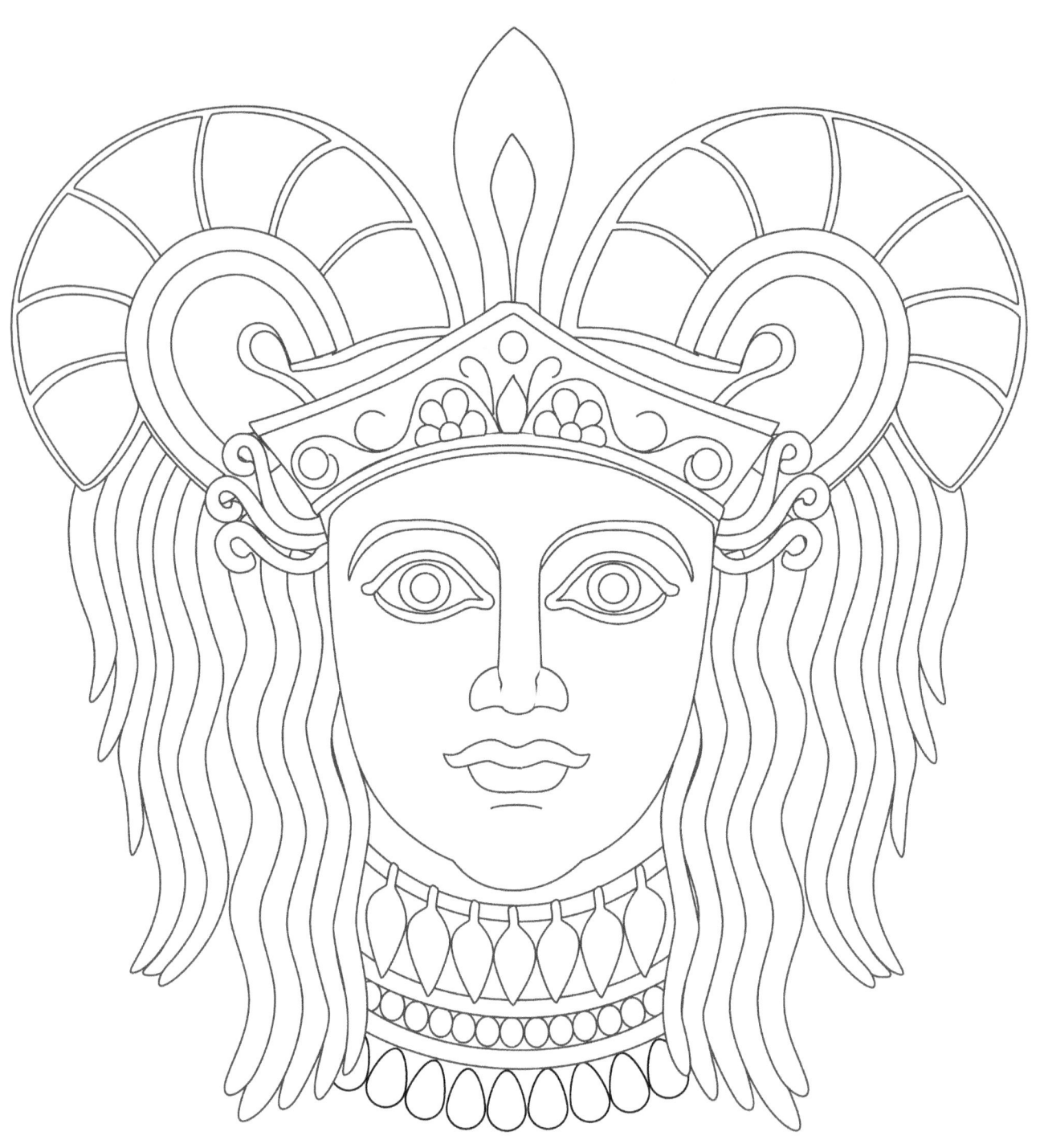

Cuirass in gilt bronze from Ksour Essaf. 3rd - 2nd Century B.C.E.

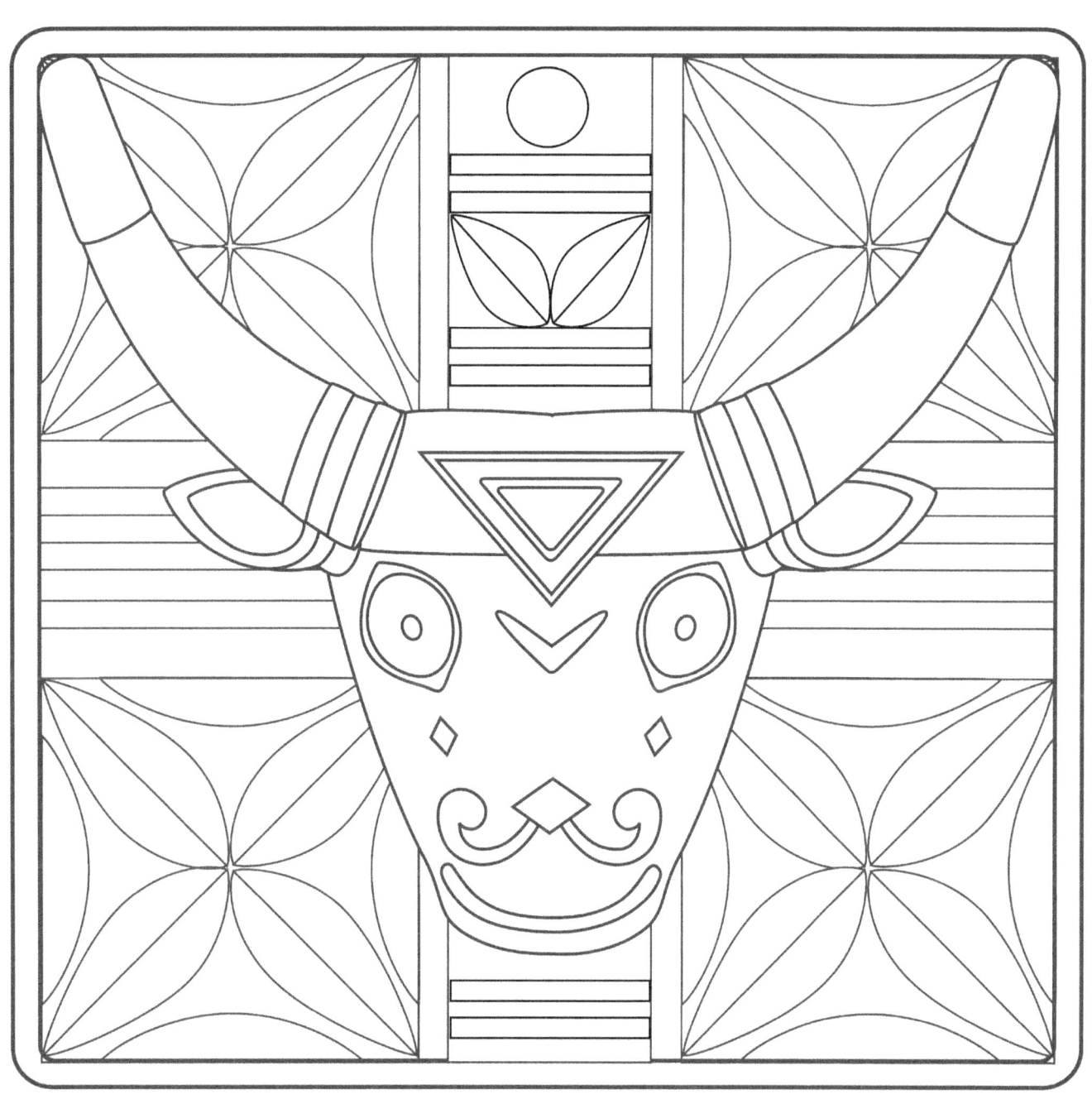

The Bull was symbolized as the God of fertility, 7th Century B.C.E.

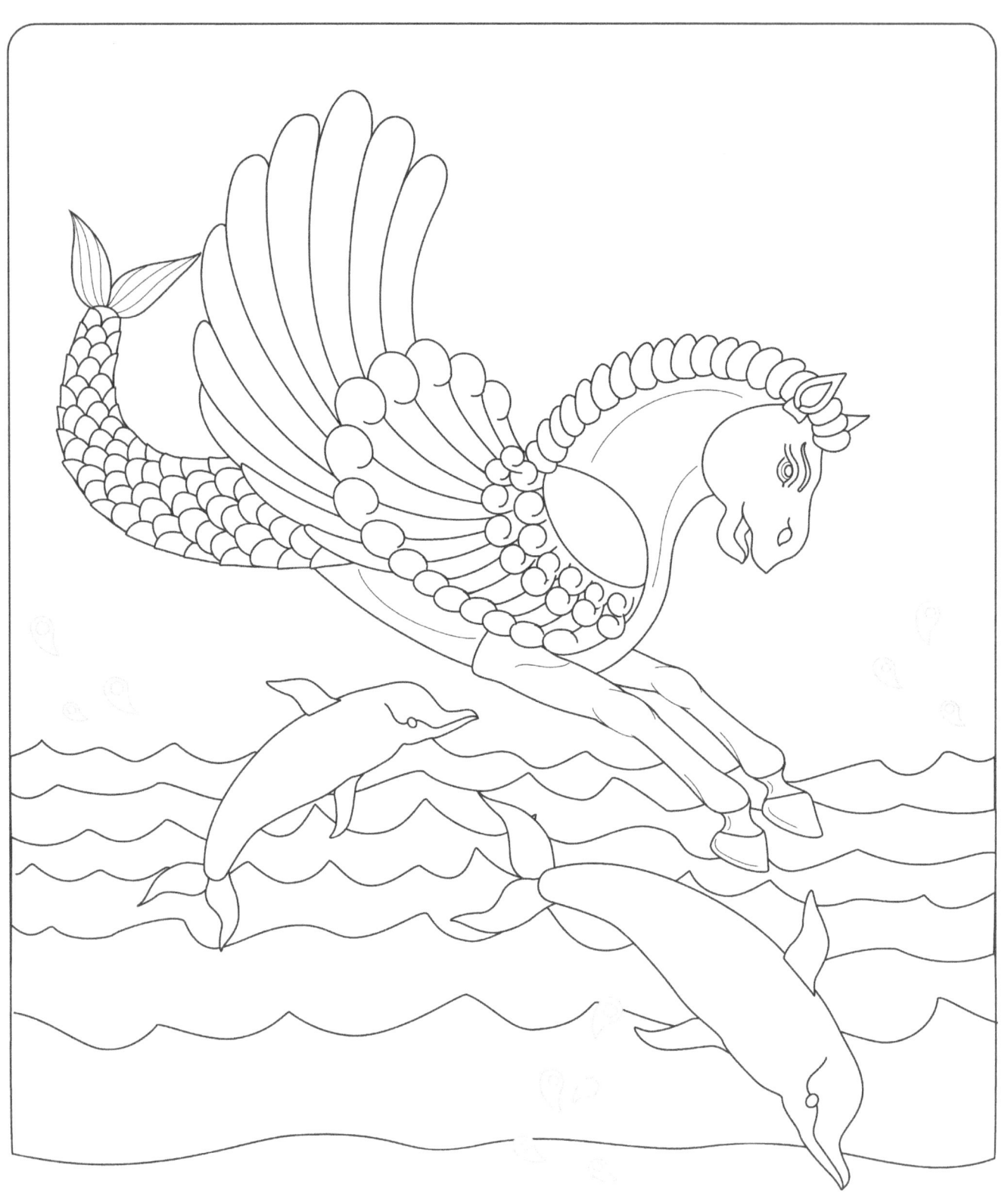

*Embossed on a Phoenician bronze coin between 377 and 357 B.C.E.
The images are of the winged sea horse and dolphins.*

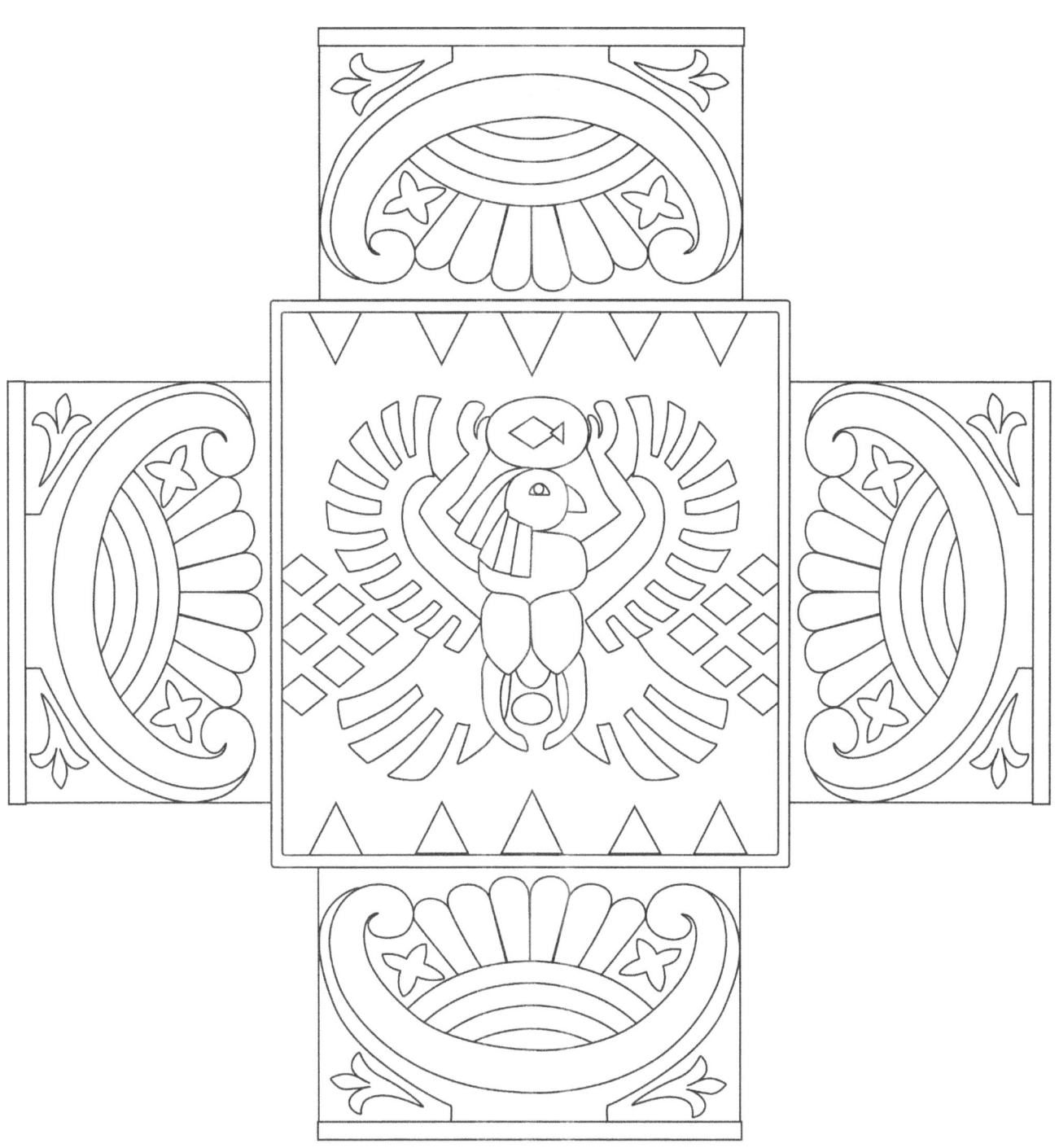

On a bracelet depicting winged beetle palmettes and lotus flowers. Tharros, 7th - 6th Century B.C.E.

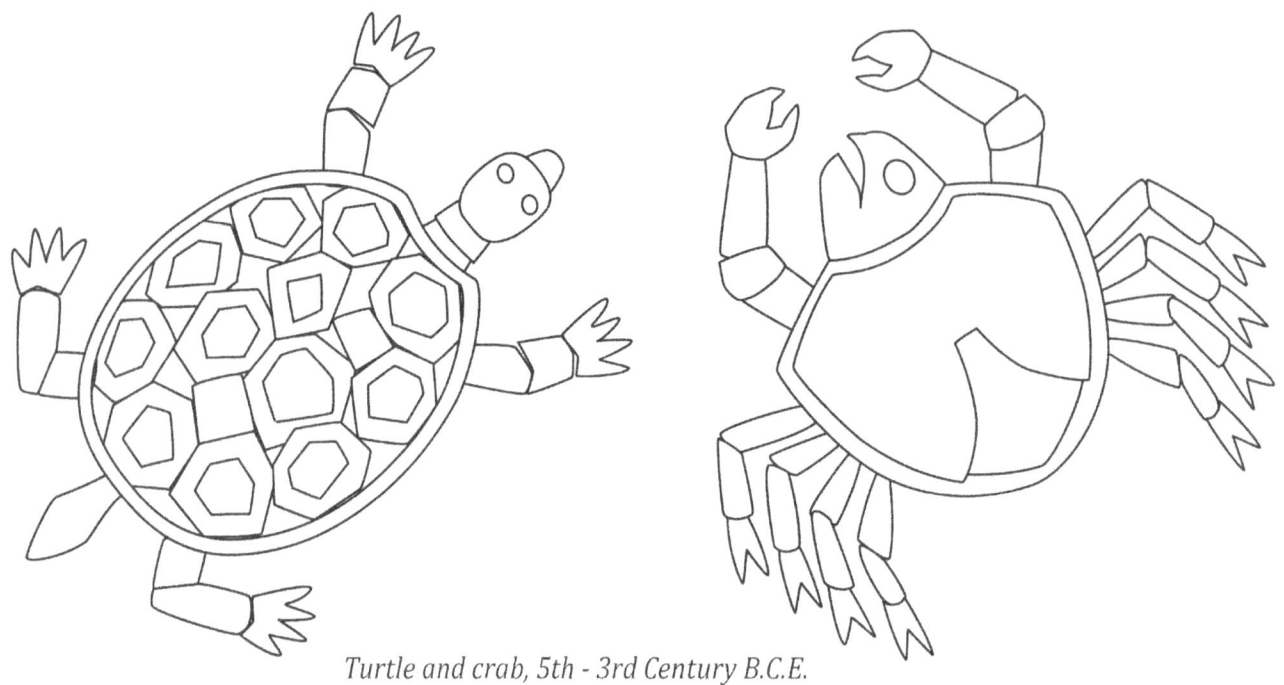

Turtle and crab, 5th - 3rd Century B.C.E.

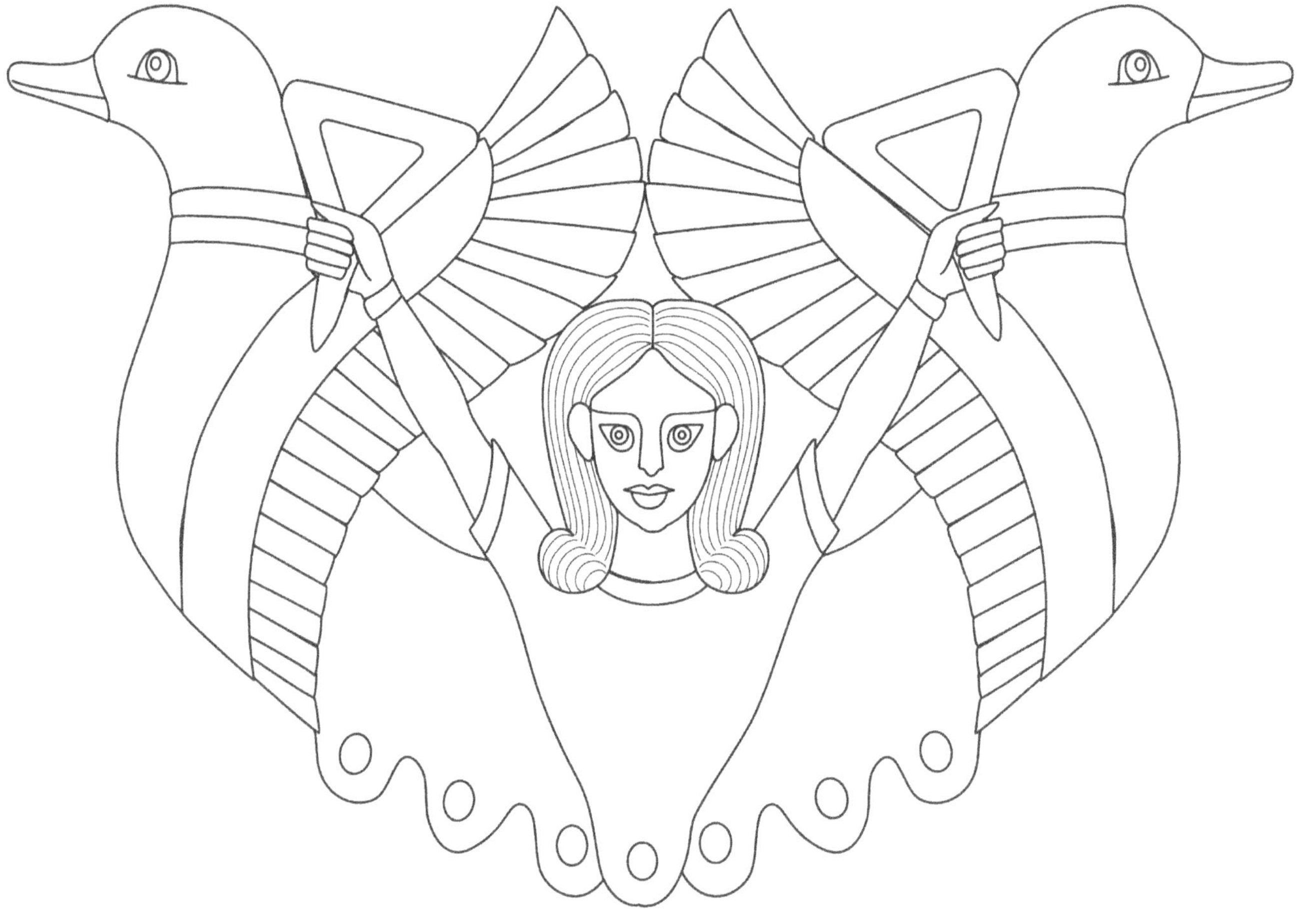

Carriazo bronze the relief plaque, representing the Goddess of fertility between two birds. Found near Cadiz, 625 - 575 B.C.E.

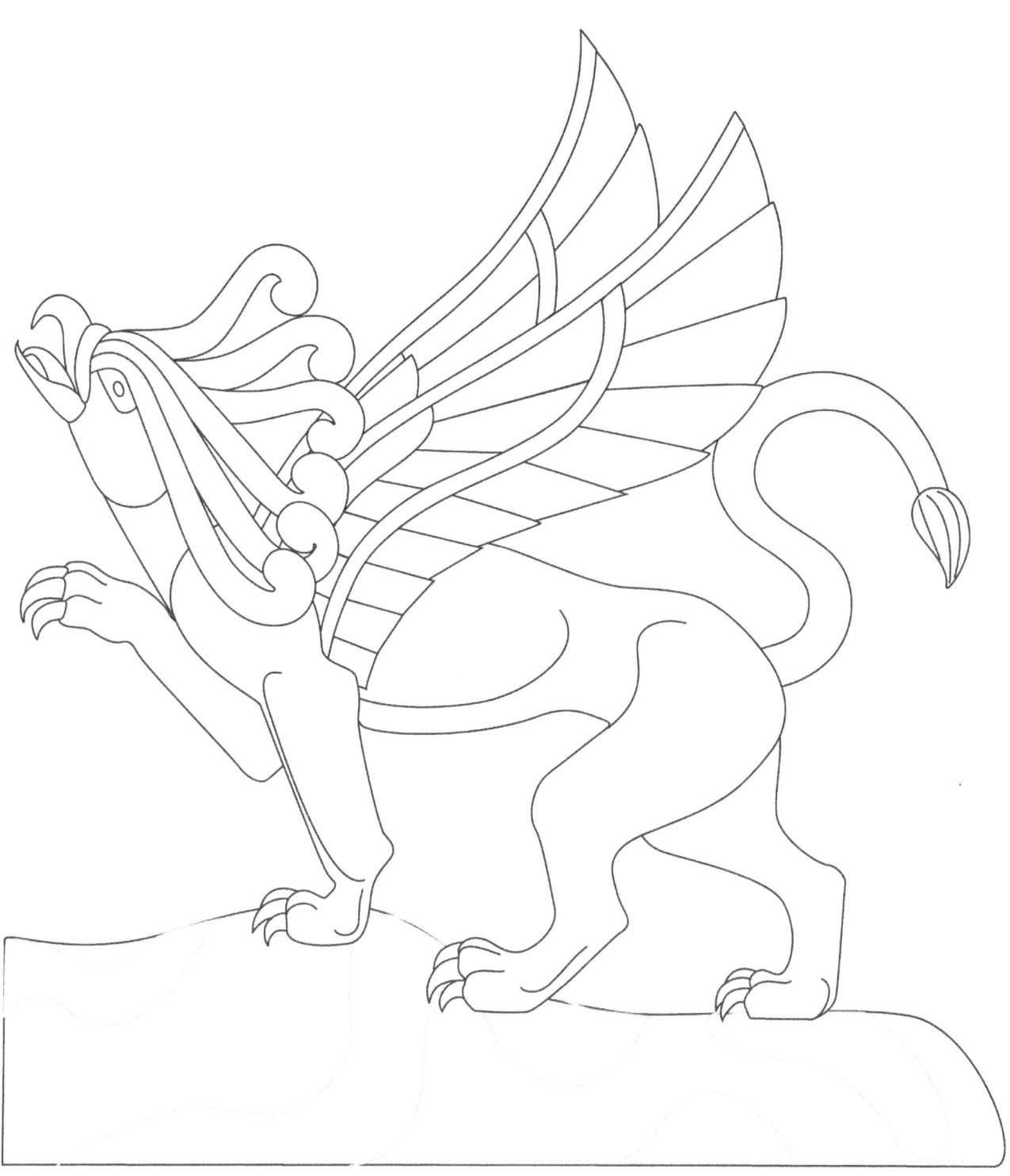

Amulet with winged Griffin from Nimrud. 6th Century B.C.E.

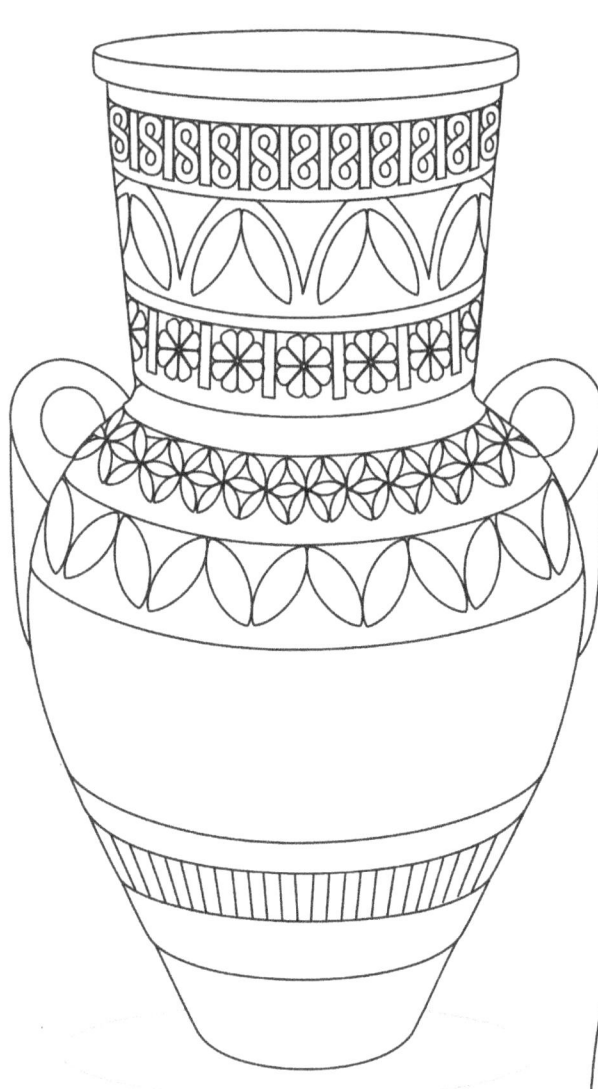

Large Amphora of the IV Bichrome.
7th century B.C.E. Nicosia, Cyprus.

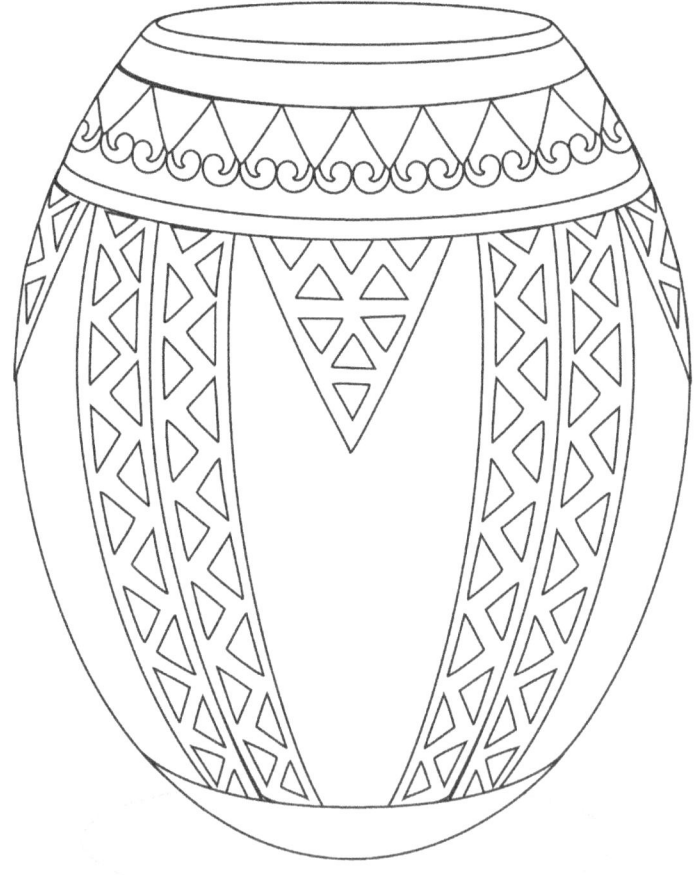

Ostrich egg cut in the form of a vase.
Metope pattern from Bithia. 7th Century B.C.E.

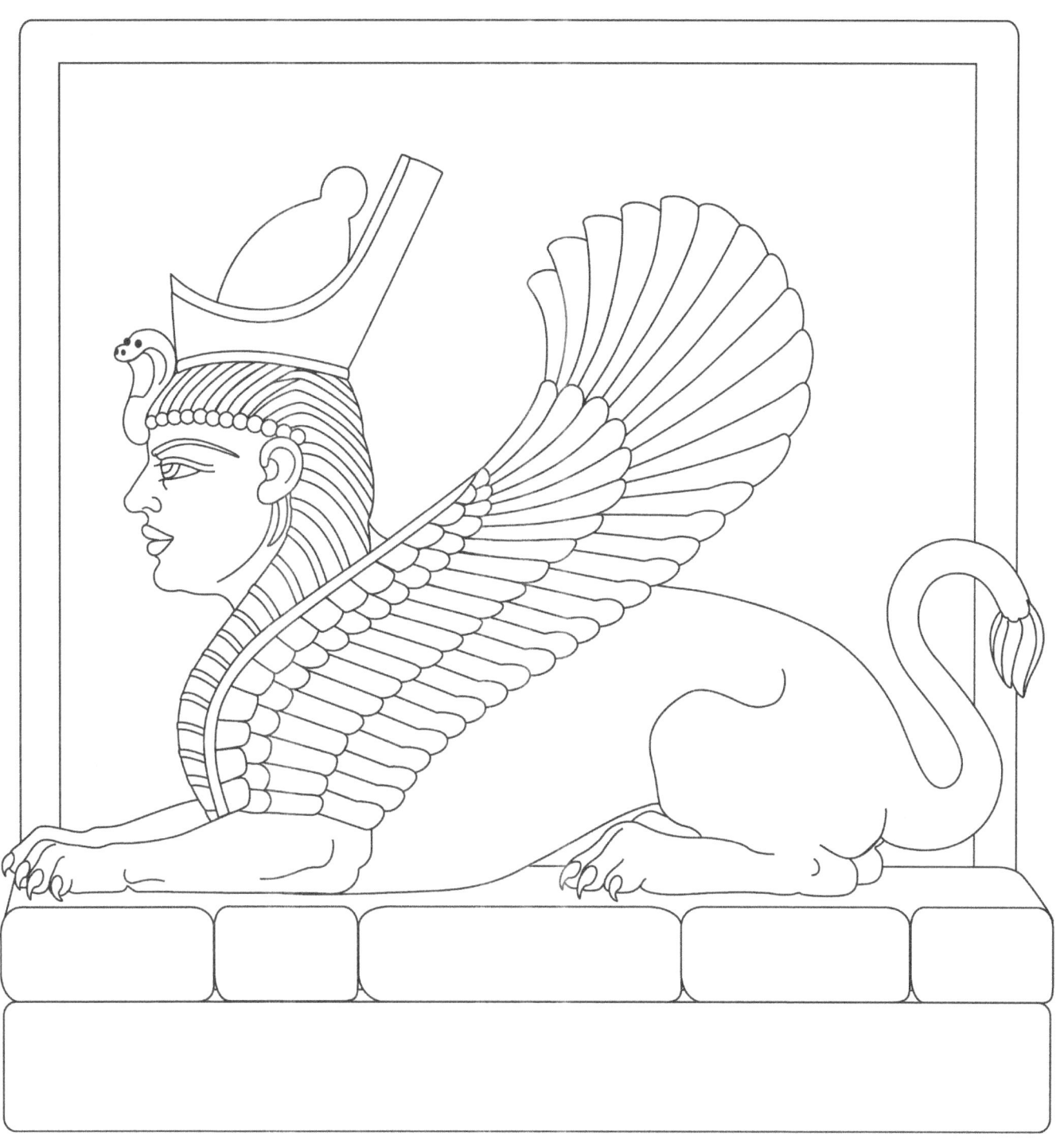

Bas-relief of a winged Spihnx on stone. Found in a tomb at Salamis, 7th Century B.C.E.

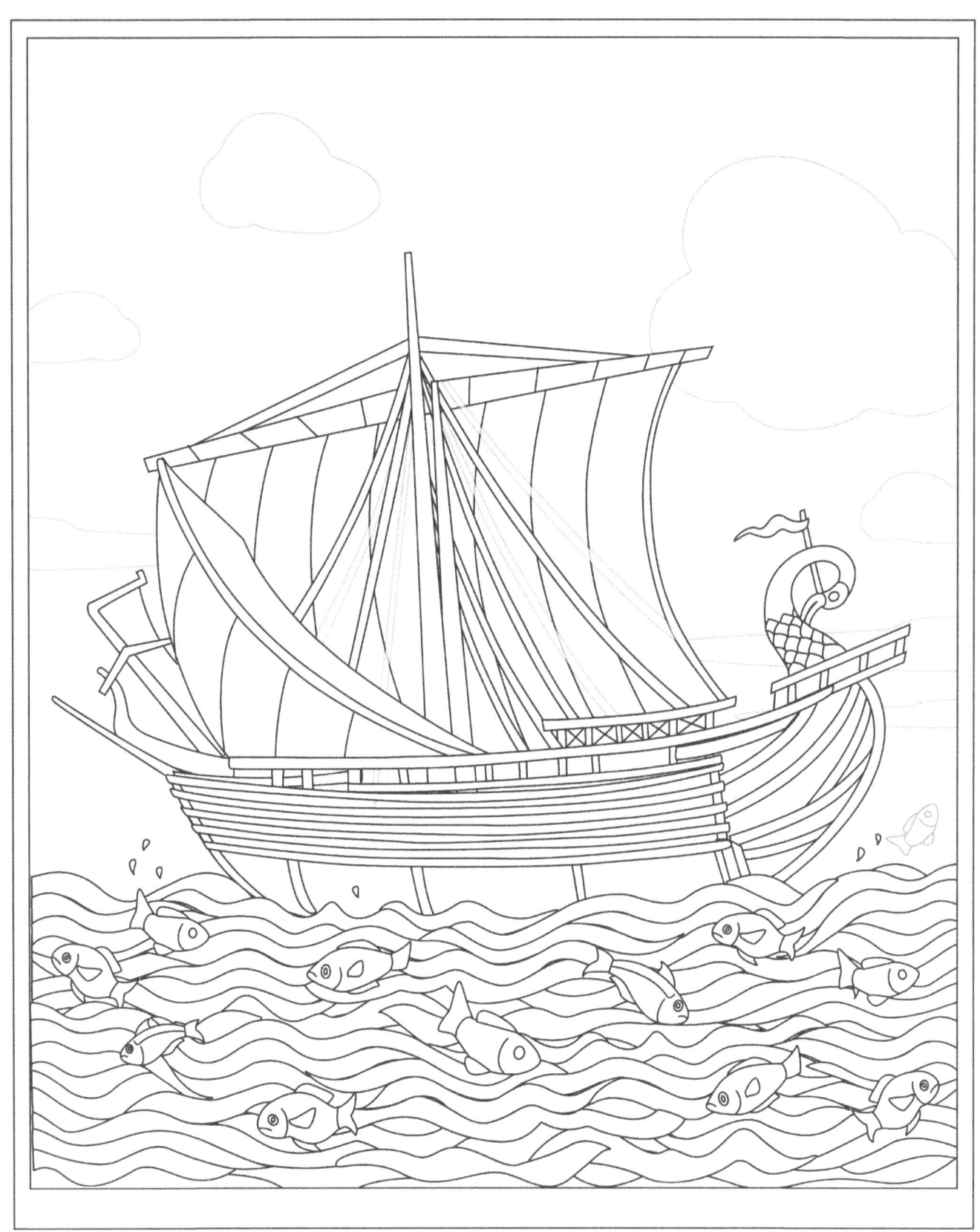

Bas-relief depicting a Phoenician trading ship, 2nd Century B.C.E.

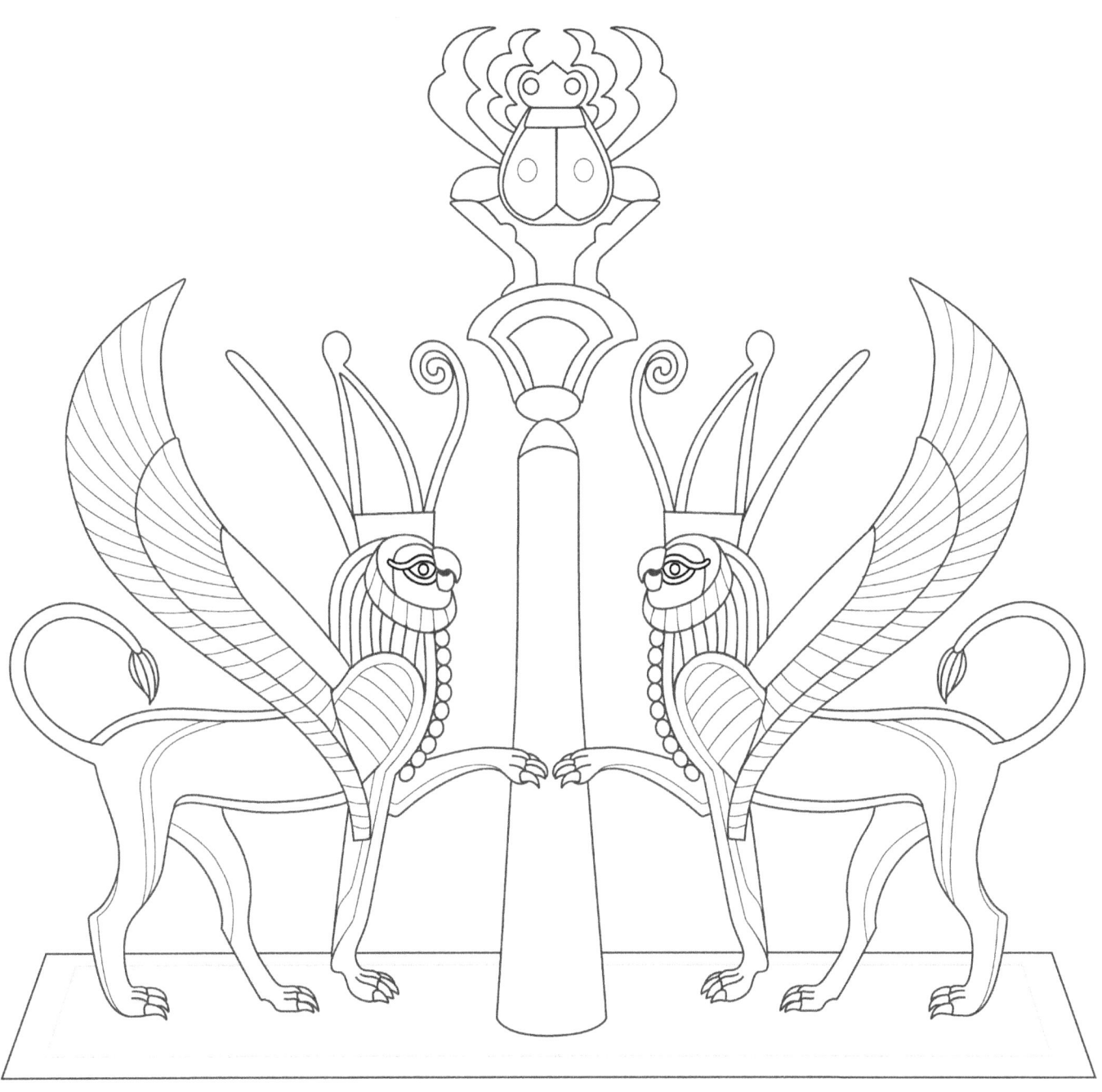

Griffins and Scarabs decorated on a bowl from Nimrud. 8th Century B.C.E.

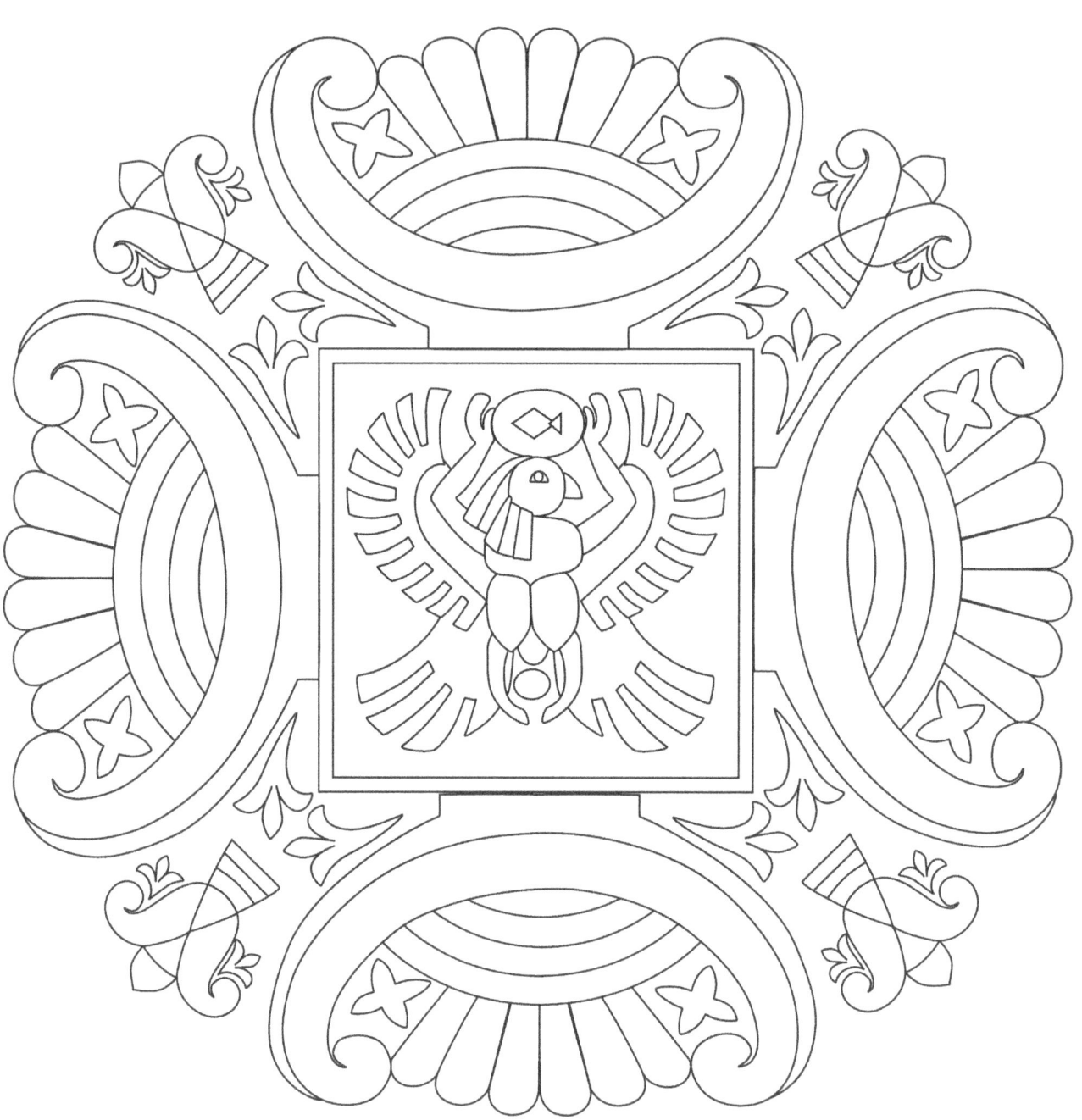

Using these images as examples, create your own piece using the elements found in Phoenician Art.

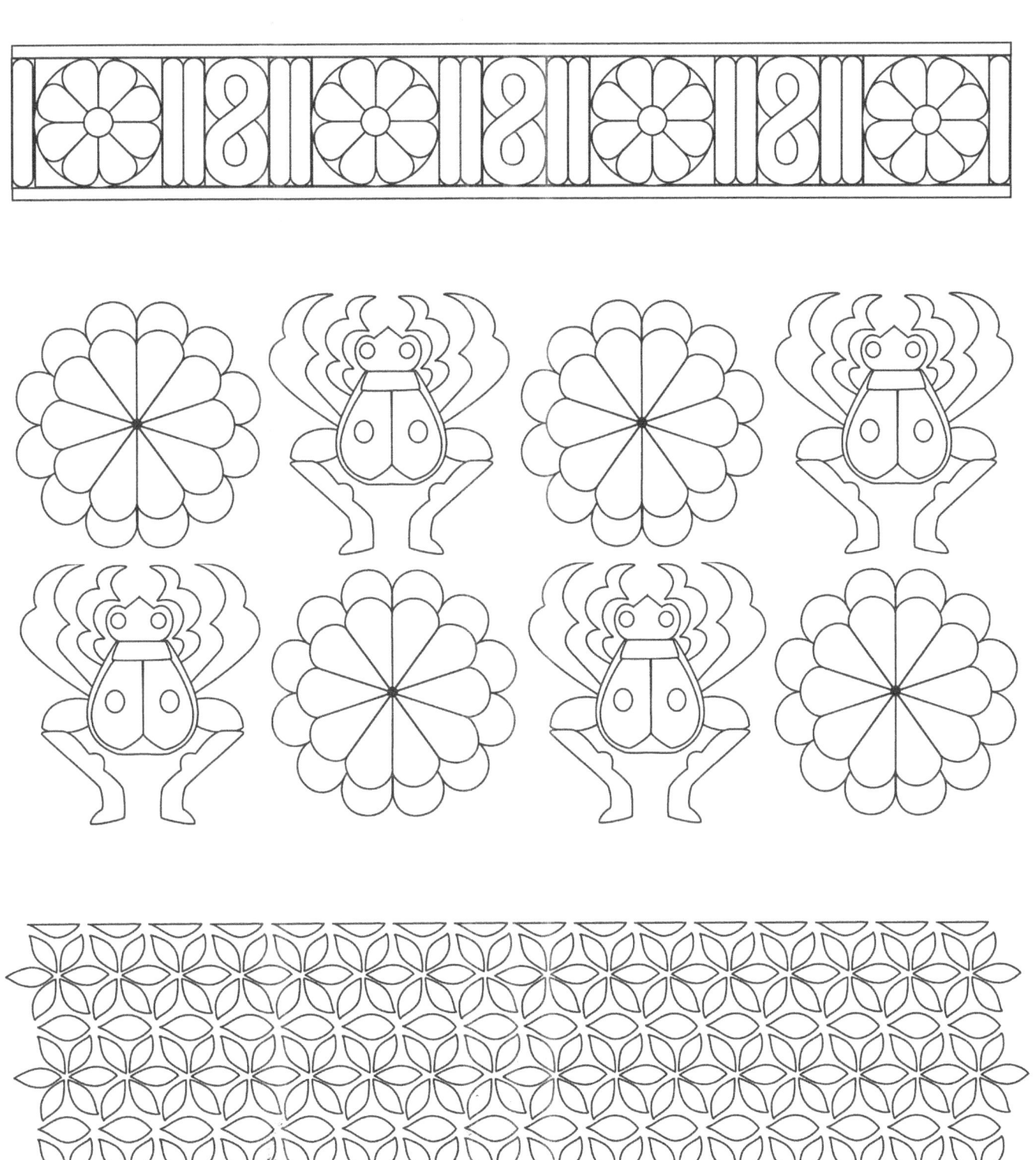

Using these images as examples, create your own piece using the elements found in Phoenician Art.

37

Egyptian art

Ancient Egyptian Civilization produced paintings, sculptures, architecture, potteries and a variety of other forms of art in the Nile Valley from 5000 B.C.E. till 300 C.E. Most of their art consists of static yet formal, as well as abstract, and is overall blocky by nature. Egyptian art reached its peak with their stylized symbolic paintings and sculptures during the reign of over 30 dynasties of the Pharaoh lineage.

Egyptian art forms are characterized by detailed depiction of their gods, people, heroic battles, nature, and their want to provide solace to the afterlife of the deceased. Art was created using a wide range of media such as papyrus drawings to hieroglyphics, and sculptures on sandstone, quartz diorite, and on granite. Egyptian art is an extraordinarily vivid representation of their socioeconomic status and belief system. Their art in unison obeyed the form of representing Pharaohs, gods, man, nature, and the environment that remained for thousands of years.

Ancient Egyptian sculptors used clay, wood, metal, ivory and stone in creating their art. Often sculptors were painted in vivid hues and had two distinctive qualities such as cubic and frontal. Egyptians were exceptionally skilled in creating pottery as well. Symbolism played an important role in establishing a sense of order. Blue represented the Nile and the life; yellow stood for the Sun God and red for power and vitality.

Artists used horizontal and vertical lines to maintain the correct proportions in their work. In order to define the social hierarchy of a situation, figures were drawn to size based on their relative importance. Pharaohs were drawn largest in the paintings, and their greater Gods were drawn larger in scale than the lesser gods. Clear and simple lines combined with simple shapes and flat areas of color helped create a sense of order and balance in the art.

Hieroglyphs may have been there since prehistoric era but Egyptians developed it as a full form of language by 3100 B.C.E., and it lasted till 394 C.E. Hieroglyphics were found everywhere in ancient Egypt, either simply incised in stone or gold, or gleaming with vibrant colors. A brilliant Englishman, Thomas Young, (1773 - 1829) did the first breakthrough and the young French scholar Jean Francois Champollion was finally successful in deciphering the Egyptian Hieroglyphics in 1822.

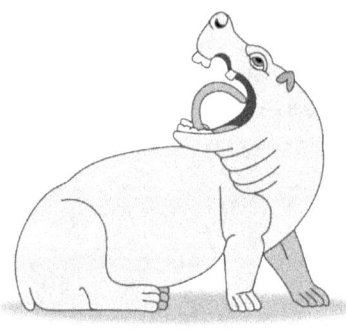

= a synopsis of =
Phoenician Art

Contrary to popular belief, this civilization used to refer to themselves as the people of "Canaanite," before the term Phoenician took its place. The word Phoenician was derived from Phoenix by the Greeks. The first Phoenician urban city emerged around 1500 B.C.E., as recorded by the Egyptians and neighboring civilizations. Phoenicians occupied the coast of the Levant (Eastern Mediterranean), and their major cities were Tyre, Sidon, Byblos and Arwad. Along with the Greeks, the Phoenicians had founded trading posts around the entire Mediterranean by the late 8th Century B.C.E. The understanding of the Phoenician culture increased significantly through countless excavations. Sea traders from Phoenicia and Carthage (a Phoenician colony founded in 814 B.C.E.), have been noted to venture beyond the strait of Gibraltar and as far as Britain.

Phoenicians created the purple dye using cedars and murex shell. Ivory was also considered as a special commodity and ivory carving was a long-established craft in their culture. Ivory items include chairs, thrones, footstools and beds, boxes and more. Ivory objects were better known than objects of silver and bronze. They were decorated with pictures of animals, mythological or imaginary creatures, hunting scenes and so on.

Records from inscriptions show that Phoenician artists were skilled in wood, glass, ivory, terracotta, metal work, and also in textile. Phoenician art is a mixture of different cultural elements with the Assyrians and the Egyptians as their predominant influence. The most significant contribution of the Phoenicians was an alphabetic writing system. Greeks adopted it and it became the root of the Western alphabets.

Artisans were often concerned with the aesthetics of the object and the purposes it could serve in both trade and religion. Their art that we find today is comprised of a variety of small objects. Phoenician art is found both in tombs and temples. Around 1000 B.C.E., Phoenician goods were found around the far corners of the Mediterranean and influenced the cultures such as the Greeks, Etruscans, North Africans and others. Artifacts were found in well-known excavated sites in Spain, Sicily, Sardinia and Tunisia and dated between 9th to 2nd Century B.C.E. Phoenician artists often used elements of Egyptian, Assyrian, or Greek, in their design and color combination.

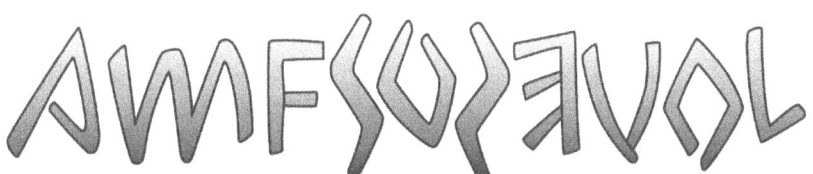

OTHER TITLES IN THIS SERIES

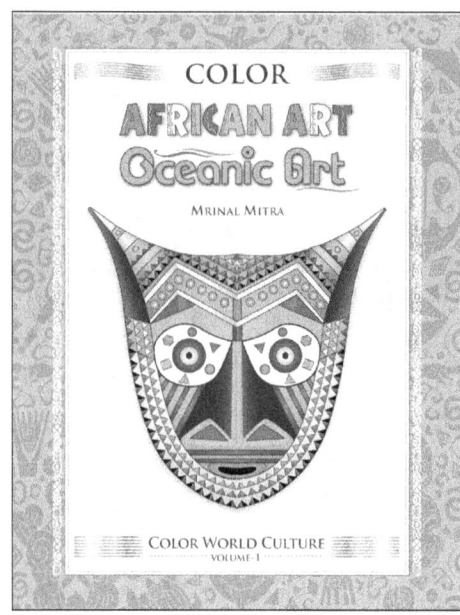

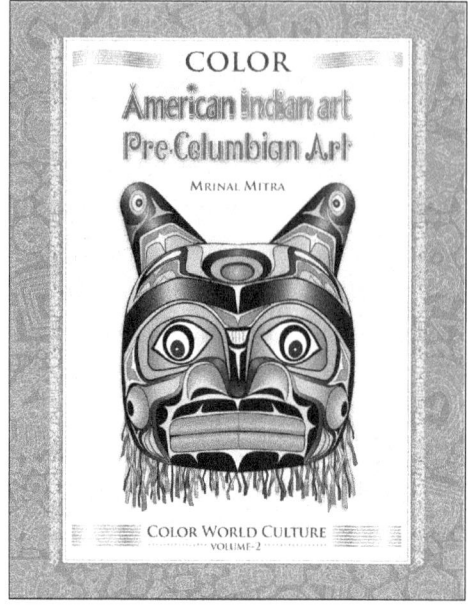

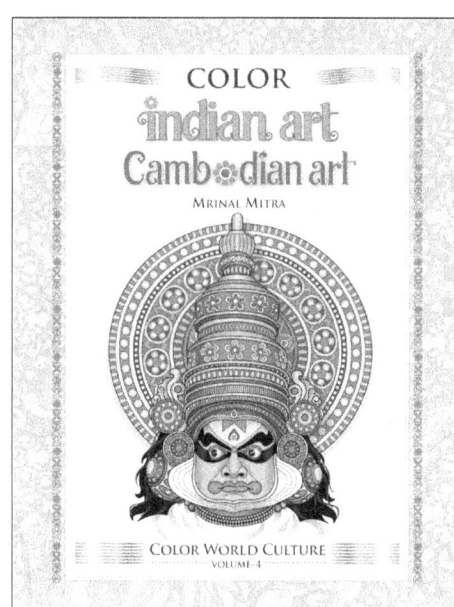

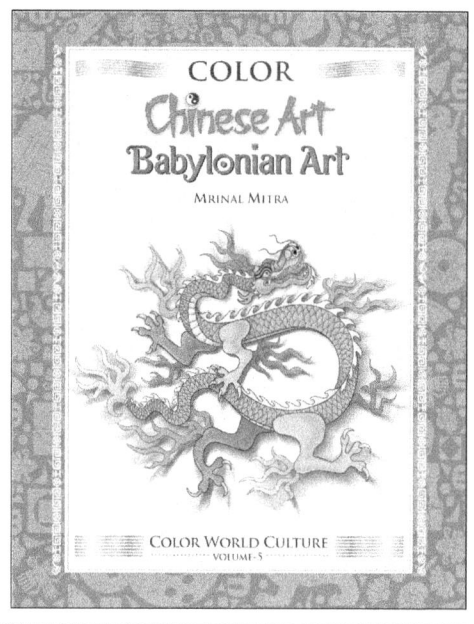

About the Author

Mrinal Mitra has earned a number of prestigious awards, both Indian and International, and received honors for his outstanding illustrations. Some of his recognitions include; The Noma Concours Award, Japan (twice), Illustrators Award, and Children's Choice Award, India, and honors from German Television "Transtel", BRNO- CSSR, TIBI- Iran, and UNICEF, New York.

Many of his talented artworks have been exhibited in several different countries such as; India, Japan, Italy, Czech Republic, Iran, and New Zealand. Mitra has authored, designed and illustrated trade and educational children's books for many Indian as well as Multinational Book Publishers around the globe.

Printed by CreateSpace, An Amazon.com. Company
Available from Amazon.com, CreateSpace.com, and other retail outlets

For further inquiry please contact Mrinal Mitra at: mitra_mrinal@hotmail.com